Powerboating
Handling RIBS
& Sportsboats
Peter White

Powerboating
Handling RIBS & Sportsboats
Peter White

WILEY ✦ NAUTICAL

This edition first published 2009
© 2009 John Wiley & Sons Ltd

Registered office
John Wiley & Sons Ltd, The Atrium, Southern Gate, Chichester, West Sussex, PO19 8SQ, United Kingdom

For details of our global editorial offices, for customer services and for information about how to apply for permission to reuse the copyright material in this book please see our website at www.wiley.com.

Library of Congress Cataloging-in-Publication Data
White, Peter, 1942-

Powerboating : the RIB and sportsboat handbook / Peter White. -- 3rd ed.
p. cm.
ISBN 978-0-470-69728-3 (pbk.)

1. Motorboats--Handbooks, manuals, etc. 2. Boats and boating--Handbooks, manuals, etc. I. Title.
GV835.W37 2009
797.1--dc22
2009008881

A catalogue record for this book is available from the British Library.

ISBN 978-0-470-69728-3

Set in Humnst777EU by Laserwords Madison, USA.

Printed in China by SNP Leefung Printers Ltd.

CONTENTS

C

1 Introduction

Powerboating is fun. The sensation of speed as you skim across the water in a fast, planing boat is terrific, and the sun, spray and sea air can all combine to make it an unforgettable experience. You will want to go out again and again, and may even buy a boat of your own. You may want to use it for waterskiing, as a dive boat or simply for transport across a big lake or between islands. You may need a safety boat with your sailing club or diving school. You may just enjoy messing about. But either way, you will need to know what you are doing.

In the UK you can purchase a boat, climb onboard and take it out without any previous experience. In most other countries you need an ICC (International Certificate of Competence). With more and more boats on the water and an increase in the frequency of accidents and near misses, many people and government bodies are calling for restrictions on use and looking towards requiring people to hold Certificates of Competence before they can use their boats. Most inland waters in the UK now require some form of certification. Insurance companies and marinas can often insist that insurance is held. That follows on from the customer holding certifates of competence. Before very long it is likely that you will have to pass a test before you can take your boat out to sea.

If you follow most of the advice in this book and practise all the exercises you will be well on your way to becoming a skilled boat handler. You should have no difficulty in obtaining a Certificate of Competence, if you need one. But more to the point, you will find that your powerboating is what you hoped it would be – fun.

If you are the skipper of the family boat, not only will you have to choose one wisely, you will also probably be responsible for maintaining it. This includes arranging adequate insurance cover, buying suitable clothing and boat equipment and making appropriate preparations every time you take the boat out. If you use the boat commercially it is vital to have a regular maintenance programme. Once again, the responsibility for this usually falls on one person.

In sailing clubs there is usually one person responsible for looking after the boats and sometimes this can be a full-time occupation.

Who is this book for?

This book is for anyone who is thinking about going afloat with a small powered dinghy, sportsboat, inflatable, small cruiser or semi-rigid inflatable boat. A comprehensive and informative handbook written by one of the top professional boat trainers in the country, it is suitable for leisure powerboaters and professionals. We recommend it as the ideal accompaniment to the RYA™ Powerboating courses.

However, the book is primarily aimed at the enthusiastic amateur who is starting out on the water for the first time. The contents will give the reader all the essential material that should, or could, be covered whilst training. Each subject opens with top tips and questions and answers intended to cover the needs of both amateur and professional users. The instructional material is easy to follow and supported by true stories.

This is a great book for anyone who believes that there is more to the subject than glancing at headings and sub headings and ticking boxes!

It is essential reading for members of water-based clubs operating safety and rescue boats.

This handbook does not claim to solve every mystery involved in boat handling but it does provide sound ideas based upon experience.

Introducing the author

Peter White has spent over 40 years on the water, of which the first 15 years were spent teaching young people to sail dinghies and training RYA Instructors and Senior Instructors. He is now a professional powerboat trainer.

Peter says, "I don't go to work. I just go boating."

1 Quick Start Guide

Pre-start checks

Before you even put the boat in the water, make sure you have:

- a suitable boat (This is not a joke. I have seen boats launched and sink.);
- protective clothing;
- personal buoyancy for everybody;
- fuel;
- fenders and lines;
- boathook and paddles;
- food and water;
- charts and tide tables,
- weather report;
- the KEYS and KILL CORDS.

Once the boat is in the water:

- Safely stow all equipment, spare fuel and ropes.
- Turn the electrics on where necessary.
- Let the crew know what you plan to do.
- Inspect engine, propeller and mounting.
- Lower the engine.
- Start engine.
- Check cooling system.
- Check kill cords are working correctly.
- Ensure there are no obstructions to the propeller.
- Test the steering from lock to lock. (Count the number of turns.)
- Decide how you are going to depart.
- Check the direction of the wind and water.
- Use kill cord.
- Look where you are going.
- Engage brain.
- Engage gear.

- **P**   Power
- **O**   Oil
- **W**   Water
- **E**   Electrics
- **R**   pRopeller

The toggle in place. Secure the other end round your leg, your wrist or to your lifejacket.

Weather
Conditions always look better when the sun is shining!

Obtain local weather reports to ensure it is safe to go out. At this stage, if in doubt, ask.

Temperature
Without the correct equipment, wind chill will significantly reduce your body temperature and inhibit your operating ability.

Rain
Rain will reduce visibility and, without appropriate equipment, can lower your body temperature and take the pleasure out of the experience

Wind
The most important factor, apart from sun and rain, is the wind, since this will determine the state of the water. Strong winds build large waves, while the direction of the wind determines the nature and effect of the waves. Wind strength is measured on the Beaufort scale. The direction is defined by the source of the wind: a westerly gale blows from the west. Wind is measured at 33ft (10m) above sea level in clear air; its strength is reduced by about a third at sea level.

A line squall, typical of a cold front or trough of low pressure in cold air.

Beaufort Force	Description	Boating Conditions	Wind Speed (Knots)
0-3	No white horses	Comfortable	0-10
4-6	White horses	Uncomfortable	11-27
7-9	Spume and spray	Dangerous	28-47
10+	Large waves and no visibility	Calamitous	48+

Try this quick reference guide to wind strength, if you know the strength of the gusts in knots: knots divided by 5 plus 1

Example   10 knots ÷ 5 + 1 = Force 3
                           20 knots ÷ 5 + 1 = Force 5

It works the other way too: shipping forecast force, subtract 1, multiplied by 5

Example   6 - 1 x 5 = 25 knots

Anything above Force 7, don't bother to subtract 1; it's a rough guide but often good enough for making passage planning decisions.

Wind and tide can combine to significantly worsen any condition.

If in doubt, don't go out.

Tides

Tides are the vertical rise (flood) and fall (ebb) of a body of water. The size of the tide is directed by the relative positions of the sun and the moon. When sun, moon and Earth are in line, we experience the highest and lowest of the tides (springs). When we see half a moon, tidal range is at its lowest and we do not experience very high or very low tides (neaps).

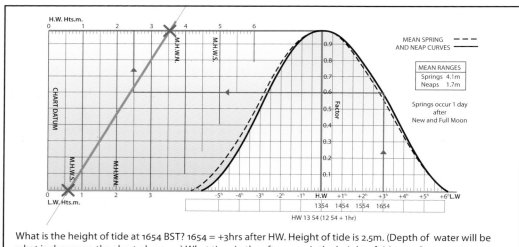

What is the height of tide at 1654 BST? 1654 = +3hrs after HW. Height of tide is 2.5m. (Depth of water will be what is shown on the chart plus 2.5m) What time in the afternoon is the height of tide 2.5m?
Answer: 3hrs after HW ie 1654 BST. (Just follow the red line the other way!)

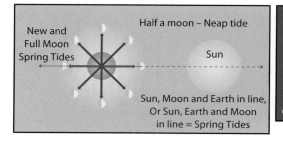

JUNE	Time	m
16	0022	3.7
	0630	0.3
SU	1254	3.5
●	1855	0.6

GMT — or adjusted for BST?

Local tide tables can be found in your nautical almanac or from the local harbour master.

High tide is at 1254 on Sunday 16 June and is 11ft (3.5m) above chart datum and it is a new moon.

Navigation

Your chart is your map at sea. Before starting out, you should understand the following principles:

- latitude, longitude and the scale and date of the chart;
- true, magnetic and compass north;
- Chart Datum (CD) or Lowest Astronomical Tide (LAT);
- transits and bearings;
- course through the water.

By using all or some of this information, you can accurately find your position on Earth.

Fixing your position

Taking bearings from three easily identifiable objects on the chart, convert bearings to true. Plot your lines – they should form a small triangle. You should be in or near that triangle. If this is not the case recheck or take a fourth bearing.

All latitude and longitude gridlines on charts are shown in true. Remember to adjust for variation and deviation.

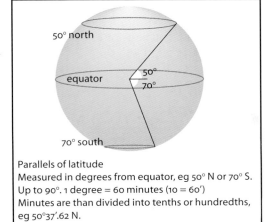

Parallels of latitude
Measured in degrees from equator, eg 50° N or 70° S.
Up to 90°. 1 degree = 60 minutes (1o = 60')
Minutes are than divided into tenths or hundredths, eg 50°37'.62 N.

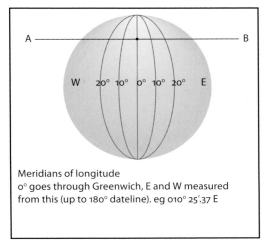

Meridians of longitude
0° goes through Greenwich, E and W measured from this (up to 180° dateline). eg 010° 25'.37 E

GPS (Global Positioning Systems)

GPS relies on communication with a number of geostationary satellites. By calculating the difference in time between the GPS unit and the satellite, your position on Earth can be accurately pinpointed. Your unit will give you a latitude and longitude reading – remember that latitude comes first. (Always remember to carry spare batteries for your hand-held GPS unit.)

Enter the latitude and longitude of your waypoint in your GPS. If you press 'Go to A', your GPS draws a line from your current position to the waypoint and gives you a bearing and distance from the waypoint.

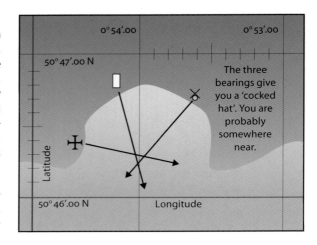

The three bearings give you a 'cocked hat'. You are probably somewhere near.

Remember:

- It will give you a straight-line course regardless of shallows, rocks or land.
- Do not make a lighthouse or anything solid a waypoint – you might hit it.

Common mistakes

- Confusing degrees and minutes, and minutes and seconds.
- Working down the page in the northern hemisphere and up in the southern hemisphere. Always increase numerically in the right direction.
- With latitude, the errors are normally east or west. For example, when travelling from A to B on different sides of the 000° line, you must input west for A and east for B. The difference is considerable.
- Recording tenths and minutes in the wrong direction. Ensure the scale is building north or south of the equator, and east or west of Greenwich.

Launch and recovery

In an ideal world, we would always launch and recover in flat water with no wind or tide, on a fairly steep, ribbed, concrete slipway. However, in the real world this is not often the case; waves, tide, seaweed, mud and wind complicate launch and recovery and it is your responsibility to plan a safe exercise. Always seek advice from local officers.

Launching on a shallow slope. *Tie a bowline around the trailer if the boat is not too heavy.*

Loop the rope around the car's ball hitch.

Allow gravity to take the boat and trailer down into deep water, the rope sliding around the ball hitch.

Launching

- Find a suitable site and check availability. Angle, width and construction are critical to a safe launch.
- Establish local protocols and bylaws.
- Position vehicle and boat out of the way of other slipway users, especially emergency vehicles.
- Remove lighting board and electric cable from the trailer and place them in the vehicle.
- Remove cover and ties from boat and engine – do not detach strop from bow winch. Also consider a separate safety strop.
- Pre-launch checks (see page 8)
- Ensure engine is tilted up on the hydraulics or locked in the up position if manual.
- Reverse to water's edge and then put one competent person onboard.
- Check depth and reverse trailer wheels into the water ensuring vehicle remains dry.
- Final checks: wind strength and direction and stream.
- In sufficient depth of water it is possible to drive the boat off and on the trailer.
- Where it is too shallow to run the engine, launch the boat and stand with it while trailer and vehicle are removed and made secure.

Recovery

Recovering the boat is essentially the reverse of launching it. If possible always put at least one crew member ashore to prepare vehicle and trailer. This person should be prepared to get wet, and should line the bow up with the trailer and connect the strop.

WARNING

A free-running winch handle can break your arm.

Manoeuvring

Driving a boat in a straight line in open water is easy. Most problems occur at slow speed in confined spaces. Creative use of wind and current can greatly simplify manoeuvres.

THREE-POINT TURN – TOP TIPS

Always spin the wheel from one lock to the other before engaging gear. You need to know the number of turns and also that the steering is free.

On a jet boat you do not have to change lock to achieve your three-point turn.

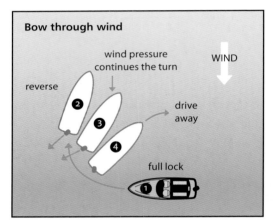

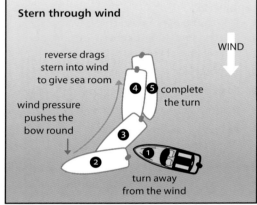

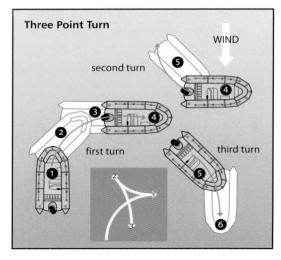

Stopping, picking up a buoy and leaving

You should aim to approach the buoy in a controlled manner and pick it up easily without using reverse gear. To do this, you have to be aware of:

Approach slowly, into the tide or wind so it stops the boat.

- wind direction and strength;
- current direction and strength;
- wind and current direction combined;
- weight of boat carrying way;
- speed of boat – most people travel too fast;
- available room to manoeuvre and escape.

To determine wind direction, look at smoke, flags, and direction of waves and ripples. Waves created by wind and undisturbed by other craft will be at 90° to the wind.

Pick up the small buoy.

To find the direction of the current, look which way the buoy is leaning and watch the swirl of water around posts and jetties – the wave pattern will show you the water direction.

To pick up the buoy:

- Stop with the buoy on the bow or alongside.
- Raise pickup by hand or boathook.
- Tie your painter to the chain or buoy using a round turn and two half hitches.

Tie your painter to the chain from the large buoy.

To depart:

- Start up procedure using pre-start checks.
- Nudge forwards or alongside using engine – don't overshoot.
- Check vicinity for clear water.
- Engage brain.
- Release painter and slip.
- Secure painter.

To leave the buoy drive up to it, cast off then allow the boat the drift clear.

Approaching and leaving a jetty

Approaching a windward or leeward jetty, always remember:

- Assess wind, tide, current and depth of water.
- Crew communication.
- Fenders at correct height and made secure.
- Lines in correct positions (tied to the boat!).
- Plan an escape route.

Downwind jetty

- Approach slowly.
- Balance boat in wind and current.
- Neutral.
- Boat drifts onto jetty.
- Secure boat.
- Plan an escape route.

Windward side (heavy wind):

- Fenders at bow.
- Attach bow spring.
- Engage forward at jetty, full lock. Gear in, out, in, out.
- Roll bow against jetty.
- Stern swings out.
- Engage neutral.
- Release spring.
- Spin wheel to opposite lock.
- Engage reverse.
- Stern swings into wind.
- Move away.

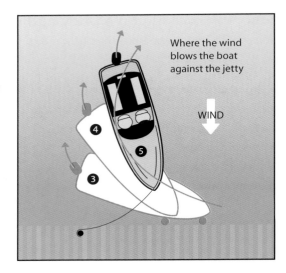

Where the wind blows the boat against the jetty

WIND

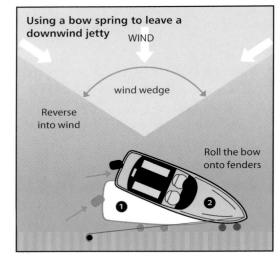

Using a bow spring to leave a downwind jetty

WIND

wind wedge

Reverse into wind

Roll the bow onto fenders

Upwind jetty

- Approach jetty at approx 20°.
- Engage neutral, allowing boat to carry way.
- Engage reverse before striking jetty.
- Pin wheel at jetty.
- Stern swings in as forward speed comes off.
- Engage neutral.
- Secure boat.
- Plan an escape route.

On leaving a jetty, always remember:

- Pre-start checks;
- Check departure route is clear;
- Communicate your plan to the crew.

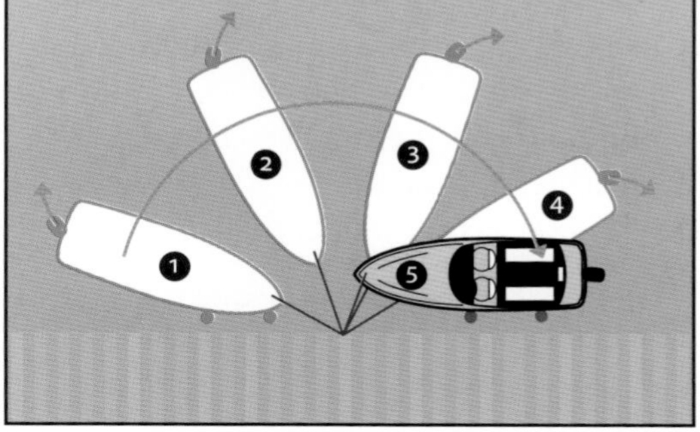

Alongside an upwind jetty

- Helm straight, gently push
- Release lines.
- Boat drifts away from jetty.
- Control boat against tide and current.

Alongside a downwind jetty (light wind)

- Similar to upwind jetty, but…
- Essential to push bow out at least 20°.
- Helm straight
- Engage gear with engine straight to protect stern of boat.

When in doubt, using the bow line as a spring should always get you out of trouble. It is important not to dawdle with the controls.

Rotating through 180° using the painter and reverse gears

First ensure painter secure and fenders in place. Turn the helm away from the jetty and if clear engage gear astern. At 4 go into neutral. If needed, spin helm to opposite lock and nudge ahead to bring the stern into the jetty. If leaving release painter at position 2 or 3

High speed

Before considering driving at high speed, check:

- Sea conditions are suitable.
- Visibility.
- Density of traffic.
- Local speed regulations.
- You have appropriate safety equipment on board.
- IMPORTANT: Remove crew from bow position and into area of safety in small boats.
- Crew are safe, prepared and happy.
- Boat is balanced.

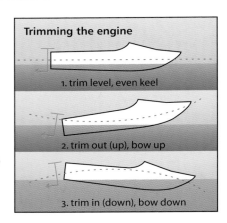

Trimming the engine

1. trim level, even keel

2. trim out (up), bow up

3. trim in (down), bow down

As you start to increase speed, it is essential that you are aware of the position of the engine, or trim tabs where fitted. A poorly trimmed engine is inefficient and could be uncomfortable or even dangerous.

As boat speed rises, ensure engine is straight and trimmed down so bow digs in, to ride the bow wave. As you increase power, the hull lifts over the bow wave, the bow wave moves towards the stern. The bow stays low and speed increases. Now trim up to lift the bow. The hull is freed to move over the water at high speed. You can now throttle back to maintain economical cruising speed.

- Always keep hand on throttle lever unless using foot accelerator.

To turn:

- One hand on the throttle, the other on the wheel.
- Look where you are turning and look behind.
- Notify crew.
- Trim down to make sure the propeller does not ventilate.
- Look again, and behind.
- Make a controlled, gentle turn.
- Increase power in the turn where appropriate to maintain planing speed.

TOP TIP

A perfectly trimmed boat is easier to drive, safer and more economical.

Knots

These are two of the most important knots:

Bowline: Can be used in most applications and will not come undone when under load. Use a half hitch to make it more secure, if left for a long period.

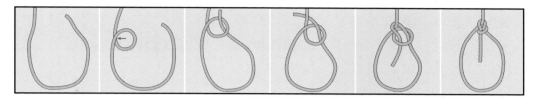

Round turn and two half hitches: Use where you need to be able to release a knot under strain. It can easily be turned into a fisherman's bend for a permanent knot.

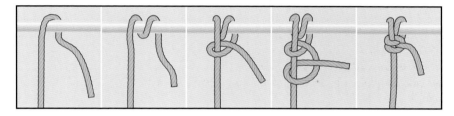

TOP TIPS

Always wash your ropes with fresh water after use and hang up to dry.

Always buy the best ropes available and seek advice.

Always carry a 6ft (2m) length of light rope. You'll be amazed at how useful it will be, whether for temporarily lashing two boats together or keeping your trousers up.

Quick Start Guide

VHF

Man Overboard

Helm responsibility

The moment you hear the shout 'Man Overboard':

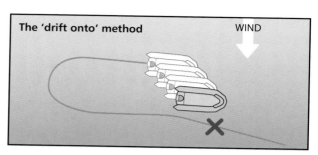

The 'drift onto' method   WIND

- Reply, 'point at casualty'.
- Hit MOB button on GPS if available.
- Make a Mayday call where appropriate.
- Get the boat under full control.
- Slow down.
- Turn towards the same side as the MOB if possible.
- Assess wind direction and determine method of approach.
- In light conditions, consider the broadside approach.
- Balance the boat across the wind, allowing time for the boat to stop naturally.
- Drift down onto MOB.
- Shut down engine 6ft (2m) away.
- Consider heaving line if boat is downwind of MOB.

MOB responsibility

Improve your chances of survival by:

- Shouting as you fall overboard, otherwise you may not be noticed.
- Closing your mouth as you hit the water.
- Inflating your lifejacket if you are not wearing a buoyancy aid.
- Keeping calm – you may be in shock.
- Remembering that in swell, you may not immediately be able to see the boat.
- Checking yourself for injuries; hitting the water at speed is like hitting a brick wall.
- Remaining still and bringing your knees together and up towards the surface.
- Holding your arms close to your sides, place your hands in your groin area – this will help you to keep warm and to survive for up to one third longer. This obviously only works if you are wearing a Personal Flotation Device (PFD).
- Watch for the return of the boat.

Getting the MOB back on board is not covered in this section due to the wide variety of techniques required for different types of boat.

Troubleshooting

The best way of making sure you don't have problems to troubleshoot is to ensure that your boat and equipment are always well maintained and up-to-date. However, there is always the unexpected.

If the engine will not start or fails whilst underway, you must source the reason. It must be mechanical, electrical or a fuel problem.

Engine won't turn over:

- No electricity – check battery, isolator switch, fuse and wiring. See if other electrical equipment is working.
- Engine may be in gear. Most should not start in gear.

Engine turns over but won't start:

- Kill cord not attached.
- No fuel.
- Stale fuel – replace with fresh or use a recommended additive.
- Fuel lines – check they are connected, and not kinked or damaged.
- Fuel pump – check priming bulb. If empty, prime.
- Water in the system – check water separator and drain if necessary.

Engine stops instantly:

- Rope round propeller.
- Electrical problem.
- Kill cord detached.

Engine falters or stutters:

- Fuel starvation.
- Engine overheating.

Steering fails:

- Hydraulics fluid – check level and leakage. If low top up.
- Cable snaps due to rust and corrosion. Strap paddles to engine outboard cover to make a tiller.

Propeller:

- Fails to turn. Old and small engines – shear pin is broken. Modern engines – thrust bearing is slipping. Replace shear pin or propeller. Potential gearbox failure.

- Vibration – damaged blades. Aluminium can be filed, gently reshaped or rebuilt. Stainless steel often needs to be replaced.
- Carry a spare propeller and the means to change it – a floating spanner. Work in a bin liner attached to the engine to catch anything you drop.

Cooling system:

- No telltale on outboard engine – check telltale is not blocked. A thin piece of wire can be used to remove blockages (hair grip or paper clip). If still blocked, remove hood, disconnect tube from inside of engine and start engine. If still no water, lift engine leg and check inlet grating is not blocked by a plastic bag. If still no water, consider a tow.

Cavitation:

- Propeller starts cavitating in a straight line with correct trim – switch off engine, lift and check for obstructions or damage around the lower leg.

Anchoring

The keys to successful and worry-free anchoring are choosing the right size and type of anchor and ensuring that you have enough chain and (sinking) rope. Your rope should be long enough to let out at least five times the depth of water at high tide. In choosing an anchor, you must bear in mind the seabed and depth of water – harbour masters are an excellent source of advice about how and where to anchor. Charts, pilot guides and almanacs include information about suitable anchorages. When abroad – see what the locals use.

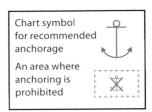

Chart symbol for recommended anchorage

An area where anchoring is prohibited

Setting your anchor in wind and current:

- Select anchoring location and check depth, traffic and hazards.
- Avoid a lee shore anchorage if you can and ensure you have room to swing at low tide. Keep clear of other boats at anchor.
- Ensure anchor is free, ready to run, marked in lengths and secured to boat.
- Select angle of approach, considering wind and current directions and strengths.
- Watch for swimmers.
- Allow boat to stop naturally and begin drifting astern or sideways.

- Communicate with the crew.
- Lower anchor and allow chain or rope to run until anchor reaches seabed.
- As boat drifts astern, let out approximately five times the water depth of rope. Mark rope to determine length let out.

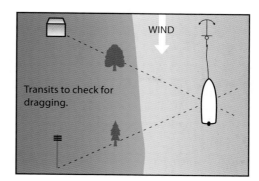

Transits to check for dragging.

TOP TIP:

If anchoring at low water, with intention of remaining for several hours, increase the amount of rope let out by five, to allow for high water.

- Allow the line to take the tension and cleat off.
- Nudge astern to confirm anchor is holding.

Ensuring your anchor is holding:

- Take transits from at least two fixed objects on the shore, such as a tree and a church.
- Recheck occasionally, (could use GPS).

Watch out for:

- Swinging onto other vessels.
- If the tide falls whilst you are at anchor, your position will change.
- If the tide rises, you may have to let out more line or reset your anchor.
- If, on recovery, your anchor is stuck, try reversing in the opposite direction or rotating astern in an arc to screw the anchor out.

Buoyage and rules

Buoys

Buoys provide information on safe passages as well as being useful navigation aids. Usually you are only likely to find extensive buoyage in areas of commercial interest; otherwise look out for innovative improvisations such as trees or scaffolding poles. Interestingly there are two different systems in use around the world. North and South America, Korea and the Philippines are in Region B; the rest of the world is in Region A.

Quick Start Guide

Quick Start
Guide

Rules

It is always your responsibility to ensure that you do not have a collision – you may have to depart from the rules to be safe, ensuring you do not make the situation worse.

- Power gives way to sail.
- A sailing vessel under engine is a power vessel.
- Power and sail give way to large vessels.
- Vessels approaching each other head on should alter their course to starboard (right) to avoid a collision.
- When power vessels are crossing, the vessel with the other on its starboard side should keep clear.
- If the vessel is on your port side, maintain course and speed. Escape route would normally be to starboard.
- You must keep clear of the vessel you are overtaking, but you can overtake either side. Starboard is the safest side because most escape routes will be to starboard.
- When being overtaken you should maintain course and speed – maintain a 360° watch.
- A sailing vessel overtaking must still keep clear.

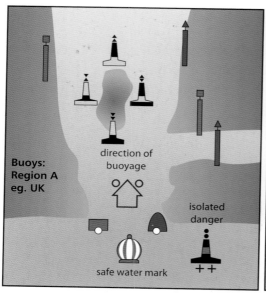

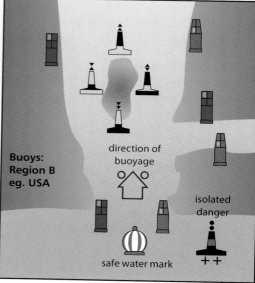

Night

Safe powerboating at night requires a sound knowledge of navigation, boat handling and crew communication and thorough boat preparation including passage and emergency planning.

You must have a well-prepared boat with:

- a large, well-lit compass;
- a hand bearing compass with light;
- GPS;
- depth gauge (sonar)
- laminated charts and Portland Plotter (you can use your fingers as dividers if necessary!);
- a sharp knife;
- a horn;
- instrumentation that can be read at night;
- a tidal curve with up-to-date information;
- a searchlight and spare batteries;
- light sticks and flares (inshore and offshore);
- lifejackets with emergency lights and EPIRBs, if possible;
- a waterproof hand-held VHF as well as fixed VHF;
- reflective strips on clothing; plus
- consider a life raft and self-righting gear for longer passages.

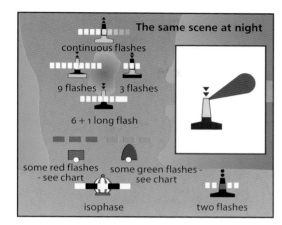

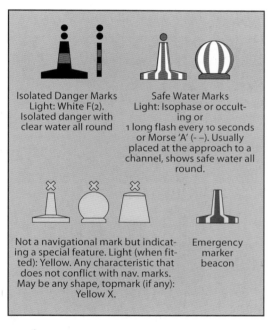

Before you depart, log the plan and inform friends and the harbour master or the Coastguard of your destination and ETA. In the UK, ensure you have lodged a CG66 with the Coastguard; it contains vital information regarding your boat and its equipment in the event of a search. Your final check should be for the latest tide and weather information.

Always try and work with at least two boats for maximum enjoyment and safety. Only consider travelling at planing speed if you have the visibility. Make sure you have practised all the relevant techniques in daylight before you attempt them at night. If in doubt, don't go out.

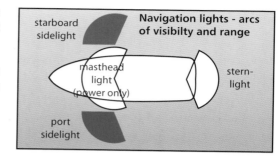

- You would not drive a car at speed, along country roads at night, without lights – the sea is no different!

Lights on your vessel
For ease of identification by other vessels, it may be necessary to display more than the minimum all-round white light. Ideally, you should display the following:

Identifying other vessels
Do not rely on others to display the correct lights, but in principle they should be displaying the following:

Under 7 m and speed under 7 knots *May show all-round white light only.*

Power-driven vessels underway (RULE 23). Under 12 m *May show all-round white light (instead of masthead light and sternlight) + sidelights.*

under 50 m *Masthead light - sidelights and sternlight.*

over 50 m *Masthead light - second masthead light aft and higher - sidelights - sternlight.*

Vessels under sail (Rule 25) *Sidelights and sternlight only - no masthead light. But small yachts (under 20 m) may combine all these into one tricolour at the masthead. A sailing yacht when motor sailing shows the same lights as a power vessel. So engine on, steaming light on.*

Vessels trawling (Rule 26) *A vessel trawling (ie towing some kind of net) shows all-round green-over-white lights. Show regular navigation lights when making way, but not when stopped.*

Vessel fishing (Rule 26) *All-round red-over-white lights, plus sidelights and sternlight (if making way).*

Getting help, distress and towing

If you have broken down and are drifting, consider your location and the conditions, the nature of your breakdown, whether you need to anchor, and how you are going to recover from your problem.

How to attract attention and get assistance:

- VHF;
- mobile phone;
- EPIRB;
- GMDSS;
- whistle;
- lights;
- flares;
- horn;
- waving arms and clothing above head;
- shouting;
- smoke.

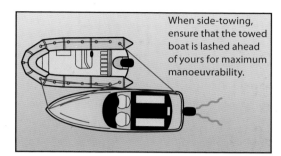

When side-towing, ensure that the towed boat is lashed ahead of yours for maximum manoeuvrability.

Watch other craft for anything unusual that could indicate a problem.

Towing

Prior to any tow, agree fees, if any – a verbal agreement made on the water is legally binding.

Long tow for use in open water:

- Ensure towed boat is far enough astern from towing boat to avoid ramming as towed boat surfs downwind.
- Crew weight to stern of towed boat to prevent veering (small boats).
- Both boats must be able to instantly release the towrope.
- Towline should be at the centre line of the towing boat or on a bridle.
- As towing boat pulls away, let off line and take up slack. Ensure all fingers are clear.
- Agree the speed of the tow.
- Communicate whilst under way.

On arrival at a marina or jetty, you may need to change to an alongside tow for use in confined areas:

- Find a sheltered area and pick up a mooring, drift or anchor
- Depending on where you plan to manoeuvre to, tow boat should attach fenders to the relevant side.

- Pull rescued boat alongside, but slightly ahead, which gives you better steerage and control.
- Attach tow boat's painter to towed boat's stern.
- Attach lines bow-to-bow and stern-to-stern.
- Prepare a spring from towed boat's bow to tow boat's stern.

First Aid on the water
DO KEEP CALM
- Get yourself and/or the boat safely to the casualty.
- Consider wind and current.
- Reassure the casualty, crew and your own crew.

DO ASSESS THE SITUATION
- Is there any danger?

- Ask the casualty and crew members what happened. Take a history.

DO MAKE THE AREA SAFE
- Make sure there is no further danger to the casualty or yourself.
- Remove the casualty from the water if possible.
- Consider hypothermia.

DO GIVE FIRST AID

More than one casualty? Treat in the following priority:
- drowning – unconscious and not breathing;
- bleeding;
- broken bones;
- other injuries.

Drowning
If you suspect the casualty is not breathing due to drowning, if possible place the casualty on their back, with their head back to open the airway. Do five inflations to clear the airway and get air into the lungs. The priority is to open the airway. Inflations can be carried out in the water.

Mouth-to-mouth ventilation

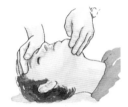

Tilt head back. Hold jaw.

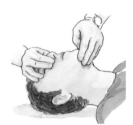

Pinch the nose

Breathe into the mouth.

Then do 30 compressions (CPR), followed by two inflations, followed by 30 compressions. Repeat sequence until casualty revives, help arrives or you are too exhausted to continue.

If you are alone, do five inflations followed by chest compressions for one minute. Then get help. Return and continue as above.

It is essential to attend a First Aid course.

Chest compression

Identify a point 2/3 down the breast bone.

Rock forward with stiff arms. Relax. Repeat 100 times per minute.

Radio distress

To really enjoy and benefit from the sport we require three ingredients:

TO GO OR NOT TO GO?
If there are any doubts in your mind, abort the trip and find something else to do.

Check and continue to check:
- weather forecast – expected;
- weather actual – what you can see and feel;
- tides – high water and low water times and direction of stream;
- assess how the wind strength and direction will react with the speed of the tidal stream or river current.

Look at other boats on the water:
- How do they lie?
- Where do they point?
- How do they lean over?
- How many boats are on the water?
- Are there any fishing boats on their moorings? If they are all in harbour, it must be dodgy.
- Any doubts – don't go out!

Personal and essential requirements:
- Clothing
- Provisions
- Drinking water

- Sufficient fuel and spare fuel
- Equipment:
- Personal flotation
- Communication – VHF ship's radio plus hand-held
- Charts and navigational information
- Satellite navigation and chart plotters
- Plotter for laying off a course on a chart, pencil, eraser
- Compass for measuring distance
- Depth gauge
- Compass and hand bearing compass
- Navigation lights and instrument lights
- Torches and personal lights for lifejackets
- Spotlights and torches for reading charts at night
- Knife and selection of tools
- First Aid kit and knowledge to use it
- Fire extinguisher/s
- Oars, paddles, boathook
- Anchor, chain and two ropes
- Ropes for towing and ropes for making secure to a jetty
- Spare ropes and a 6ft (2m) light line
- Throw line and bag
- Exposure bag for someone who is cold
- Warm drink and food – no alcohol

Ready to go:

Have a passage plan

Inform friends where you are going and when you plan to return.

Consider CG66 form

Now recheck the weather!!!

- Remember: there is no such thing as 'popping out to sea for five minutes'! Always ensure you carry at least the essential equipment from the above list.

2 Which boat?

The first step towards enjoyable powerboating is choosing the right boat. It must be suitable and safe for the type of water in which it will be used. Some boats are designed for flat water, while others are specifically designed for coastal waters and the open sea.

If you are going to use the boat for pleasure then it must be fun and easy for two people to handle. If it is to be used for commercial purposes, it must be functional and safe.

Too many people buy a dream and in doing so, lose sensibility. Always go out in a boat *before* making any financial commitment. Would you buy a car without first taking it for a test drive?

The hull

The nature of a hull will determine how a powerboat performs in various types of water and at different speeds. This, in turn, influences suitability for the activities you have in mind.

Displacement craft

Displacement craft sit in the water. The waterline length governs the speed of the hull through the water. They generally handle well and have good directional stability forwards, but going astern creates very heavy pressure on the rudder and steering is very difficult. Many such boats will travel in only one direction astern because of the paddlewheel effect of the rotating propeller.

Comfortable boating but can roll in a cross sea.

The speed of displacement craft is not unduly affected by the weight of the load, although they should not be overloaded. Their construction is usually robust and they will handle heavy weather quite well. Balance and trim are not of vital importance. They generally have inboard engines, and are left on moorings.

Planing craft

A high-speed planing craft relies upon a large power unit installed in the hull to push it from displacement mode up onto the plane. As the power increases, the hull is forced to ride the bow wave. With even more power the bow wave

Author pushing a race boat hard on flat water.

2

moves back towards the stern of the craft, so there is less hull in contact with the water and less resistance. As the boat flattens out on the water the speed increases and the engine can be throttled back. Maximum speed depends on the shape and weight of the hull, engine, fuel, equipment and crew, as well as the wave height and wind strength.

A flat hull travels faster than a deep V-shaped hull because the 'V' cuts through the water, whereas the flat hull skims across the surface. However, a flat hull can only be used on flat water. If it rides waves, it will shake itself and the crew to pieces.

The best compromise is a hull with a deep 'V' at the bow, but becoming flat towards the stern. The deep 'V' parts the water at the bow and directs this water towards the flat area at the stern, which skims over the surface. The angle of the 'V' and the rate of flattening towards the stern vary from hull to hull, depending on the conditions the hull is designed for. It is important to choose the best design for the waters you will be using.

You may have heard the terms dead rise or flare. They refer to the angle between the hull and a horizontal line drawn through a cross-section of the keel.

A conventional high-speed planing hull relies upon a dead rise at the bow of approximately 45° diminishing to an angle of 15–22° at the stern. This combination cuts through the waves and provides a reasonably soft ride. The main lift point occurs around the longitudinal centre of gravity, so the most critical factor affecting the planing performance of the boat is the angle of the hull aft of this central point.

Catamarans

Catamarans are becoming more popular as high-speed craft than they ever were before. The two hulls side by side reduce the drag effect of a large hull under the water. Stability can be improved due to the overall width of the hull and the speed increases because there is less hull resistance through the water.

Cathedral hulls and dories

Smaller dories are designed for planing in moderate conditions and are ideal for sheltered

Solar powered twin hull – Chichester Harbour Conservancy Watertours

waters. The dory is often the choice of inland sailing clubs because it is double-skinned with built-in buoyancy, enabling the boat to stay operational even when swamped. Dories make ideal platforms for carrying heavy loads, and are excellent workboats. They have good directional steering at slow speeds but can be very uncomfortable when travelling fast in large waves.

Nevertheless, some of the more recently designed large dories, similar to the Boston Whaler, will tolerate heavy conditions and are able to carry large payloads at very high speed. Many used by the military can achieve more than 40 knots and carry heavy loads.

V-hulls

A V-hull craft has poor stability when at rest, but this improves dramatically when the boat is moving fast through the waves. A deep 'V' gives a soft ride because it cuts through the lumpy water. In general, the shallower the 'V', the harder and less comfortable will be the ride.

Buoyancy is built into some craft. If not, some buoyancy should be put in for safety. If the hull is long enough, you can choose between an outboard or inboard engine. Performance craft are often fitted with outdrives. Good balance and trim are essential.

Small 'Boston Whaler'

2

Semi-rigid inflatable boats (SRIB)

These combine the benefits of rigid high-speed hulls and inflatable side tanks, offering speed plus soft contact with other boats, or people in the water. This makes them excellent rescue craft as well as fun boats. They possess a massive amount of buoyancy and can carry heavy loads, although balance and trim are essential to good performance. Their seaworthiness is excellent in heavy weather, although the crew can become very wet. Many have self-draining cockpits.

Police recovering their search and rescue RIB (dive unit).

RIBs can be fitted with single or twin outboard or inboard engines. Water jet engines can be fitted to these boats, which are best used with trailers or launching trolleys, although they can be left on moorings.

When 24 ft (7.5m) and upwards, RIBS are sometimes fitted with inboard diesel turbo engines, giving a very fast ride in exceptional comfort. Although the engines are expensive to purchase in the first place, the fuel economy is exceptional.

Inflatables

Inflatables are entirely constructed of rubber-type fabric. Some have separate inflatable sections for the hull which, when pressurised, performs in a similar manner to that of a semi-rigid inflatable. These are very fast, very wet boats, often with excellent directional stability at high speed. At slow speeds they are greatly affected by the wind.

2

Inflatables are capable of carrying heavy loads and are extremely buoyant. Again, trim and balance are essential for good handling.

Inflatables are usually fitted with an outboard engine or engines. Very few boats are left on moorings overnight and therefore need a trailer or trolley.

Tenders
A small inflatable, fitted with a small outboard bracket and engine, makes an ideal tender for a larger craft. It is excellent for short rides between shore and boat, and can be deflated and stowed in a bag easily and quickly, making a trolley unnecessary.

Author and Tracey Edwards, charity event, London canals.

Pram dinghies
These are excellent for single-handed launching and recovery and for getting out to a moored boat. Some have a wheel built into the bow and two oars making the handles. They should really be called a wheelbarrow dinghy.

Family river pottering. Note the correct attire: buoyancy and life jackets.

3 Which engine and trailer?

Most small sportsboats use outboard petrol (gasoline) engines. Diesel outboards are available, but they are more expensive and very much heavier for the same power. Electric outboards powered by a rechargeable battery are used on small dinghies. Where quietness, economy and cleanliness are the keynote, four-stroke outboards take some beating. Whatever type of boating you plan to do, the power unit is out there somewhere.

For a larger boat you might choose an inboard engine. This may be a petrol (gasoline) engine – probably a marinised car or truck engine – or a diesel. Some have simple shaft drives with rudders for steering, but these are not recommended for general-purpose boats.

Really powerful craft may have twin engines, which give you extra flexibility when manoeuvring.

Outboard or inboard?

A power unit fit for the job

Always have a large enough engine to cope with the task you have set it. A small engine will be used flat out nearly all the time, whereas a larger one will be used at three-quarters of its maximum output. However, an outboard engine enjoys working hard and often. It dislikes being left under a damp cover for weeks and weeks without work. An engine that is well used and well maintained by a professional engineer will work for thousands of hours. If abused, it may be destroyed instantly on day one.

Easy to change an outboard, but, to my knowledge, an outboard doesn't run a heat exchange unit for taking a shower.

Propeller

Propellers are made from a variety of materials. Outboards and small sportsboats usually use aluminium propellers, which are reasonably priced and very efficient. Used correctly, their life expectancy will be long. However, I have managed to wear out a propeller after 3,000 hours of use.

The blades of a propeller can be destroyed in seconds if the engine is put into gear when its lower leg is sitting on shingle, rock, a wooden slipway or concrete. Even if it is not completely wrecked, the propeller can be put out of balance if a large piece is missing from one blade. Used at speed, it will cause vibration that may harm the engine and the gearbox.

Propellers can have several blades. Here is a 3-blade propeller, other models can have 4, 5 or more.

If the damage is minimal, an aluminium propeller can be rebuilt, which is cheaper than replacing it. When repaired skilfully, the propeller can be as good as new.

Types of trailer

Road trailers

Do use a trailer recommended by the manufacturer of the boat, designed or adapted to fit the boat concerned. It must offer maximum support to ensure safe trailing, launching and easy recovery from a variety of sites.

Small powerboats can safely be carried on two-wheel trailers. However, depending on the weight of the boat, the size of the towing vehicle and the legal requirements of the country in which you are towing, the trailer may be required to have brakes. The unbraked weight of a trailer in the UK is 1,653lb (750kg).

Heavy craft should be transported on braked, four-wheel trailers. Dealers and manufacturers can advise on the most suitable equipment.

The road trailer must be strong enough for the boat and maintained in good condition. It is costly, embarrassing and possibly very dangerous, if a trailer collapses while it is being towed along the road.

Road trailers are often used for launching into deep salt water. Salt water is very corrosive. Ideally, if you keep the boat on dry land close to the launching site, use a separate launching trolley. Your road trailer will last far longer.

Current UK regs:				
Cars towing trailers or caravans	Built-up areas	Single carriageways	Dual carriageways	Motorways
	30mph	50mph	60mph	60mph

3

Breakback trailer

This is a trailer designed for launching and recovering a boat without immersing the wheel bearings in the water. The success of this depends on the skill of the person doing the job, coupled with the angle of the slope at the launching site. If the angle is too shallow, the boat will slide off the trailer and the transom will hit the ground. Breakback trailers take some getting used to, but they can be very effective in the right circumstances.

A well-balanced trailer is a joy to drive.

Road trailers in salt water

I do not like immersing trailers in seawater but find it unavoidable. The problem with a braked unit is the salt water remaining inside the wheel and brake hubs. After every immersion you should strip down and clean the hubs and check cables etc. This becomes an onerous task when the trailer is being used regularly.

Never leave a trailer with the brake lever in the on position – especially after a dunking – even for a short time. The brakes will stick in the on position and, although you may have released the handbrake on the trailer, the brake shoes will not release and will remain stuck on. After a few miles on the road the braking effect of the trailer will be nil. Chock the wheels if on a slope and then release the brakes.

There is a system for washing the inside of the brake hubs.

4 Getting afloat

A boat is no use without water to use it on, and the water has to be the right type!

Rivers

Many small rivers and canals are only suitable for sedate boating in low-speed displacement craft. The charm of such boating lies in the beauty of the surrounding countryside, and having the time to stop and appreciate it. This type of boating is very relaxing, but can involve numerous problems that are not immediately obvious. These include avoiding weirs and shallows, negotiating locks, overhanging trees, low bridges and cables, and keeping clear of shallow sections on the insides of bends. Most rivers and canals display speed limits and, on the whole, fast powerboats are not welcome unless they are just 'gurgling' along. Some larger rivers may have designated high-speed areas suitable for planing craft, and water sports.

Lakes

Inland lakes and gravel pits offer a totally different boating environment. Many are now being used for a combination of water activities, including jet biking, waterskiing and powerboat racing. For safety reasons, use of the water is generally tightly controlled, with a limited number of craft allowed on it at any given time. Users must stick to a specific circuit route, and club membership and training are necessary before going afloat.

Mic Randle and the author working on the Personal Watercraft training scheme.

Reservoirs

Reservoirs are not really the domain of powerboat users. They are frequently used by sailing clubs and fishermen and often include sections set aside as nature reserves and bird sanctuaries. Unless you belong to a club, you are unlikely to obtain permission to use a reservoir.

Estuaries

Estuaries often look quiet and peaceful, owing to the shelter offered by the surrounding land, and they usually offer excellent sites for the launching and recovery of powerboats. However, you must always beware of potential hidden dangers.

Coastal waters

A whole book could be devoted to this topic. Basically there are some stretches of coastline that are ideal for powerboating and other stretches where it would be far too dangerous to venture out. Yet it is not always obvious which is which.

Local knowledge is essential, but how do you obtain local knowledge in the first place? Start by studying this book, together with an up-to-date chart of the area. Then sign up for a training course with a recognised powerboat school. This should set you up for your future life on the water and local knowledge will be quickly gained thereafter.

Ask yourself the following questions:

- Do many people use this stretch of coastline for sailing, windsurfing, yachting, fishing or waterskiing?

- Is it busy?

- Are there any harbours or bolt-holes where a boat can seek shelter if the weather deteriorates?

- Do these harbours offer any refuelling facilities and good launching and recovery facilities?

- If you can answer 'yes' to these questions, then this is likely to be a suitable coast to explore with your powerboat. But if the waves are pounding on the shore and there is nobody in sight, then I suggest you go elsewhere.

Offshore waters

You should only venture offshore in a small powerboat if the conditions are ideal and the weather forecast is favourable. Your boat must be well equipped, you must plan the journey carefully and you should never attempt your first trip alone. Yet, despite all this, a journey of over 100 nautical miles out of sight of land is not unrealistic for a fast, powerful craft in the hands of a competent crew.

Where to launch

There are generally three main ways of getting access to the water:

- obtaining permission to use a private site;

- relying on public amenities;

- launching off the open beach.

Private launching sites

Some private sites are owned by individuals, but most are the property of recognised clubs and marinas. Do visit your local marina and speak to the manager. I usually find the staff most helpful, especially if you explain that you are new to powerboating.

Robert Owen Marine, Porthmadog now use a crane for launching.

Facilities on offer usually include a yacht club, chandlers (for the purchase of ropes, flares, electronic equipment etc), restaurant and other shops.

Some marinas let you handle your own launch and recovery while others have their own equipment with professional staff operating it. This equipment might consist of four-wheel drive vehicles, tractors or hydraulic lifting forks, which are designed to lift a boat from the shore and lower it into the water alongside the pontoon. Some marinas use purpose-built hoists. Recovery is effected in the same manner. One advantage of joining a marina is that you can often store the boat on site, which saves trailing. When storage space is at a premium, sportsboats can be safely stacked in racks, one above the other.

All this costs money, of course. Trailing the boat to a public site is cheaper, but often it is a more difficult option.

Public launching sites
As the name implies, these are for the use of the public, for launching and recovering any waterborne craft that are permitted within the local rules and regulations. This may include dinghies, powerboats, canoes, jet bikes and fishing boats. Most are very well maintained and offer excellent facilities, including water for washing down at the end of the day. You must expect to pay a fee – payable daily, weekly or annually – for the use of these facilities, but it may work out cheaper than joining a club.

Open beaches
Launching and recovering a powerboat on an open beach is possible, but often difficult. Success depends on several factors:

- how you reach the shore;
- the type of access;
- the firmness of the shore;
- the slope of the beach;
- the available depth of water.

If all these are suitable, you still have to give consideration to the wind strength and its direction.

Large waves breaking on the shore indicate a strong onshore wind that makes launching the average sportsboat virtually impossible. It only takes a small wave to lift a hull clear of the trailer. Even swell can cause a problem.

Suitable rescue craft managed by sailing clubs can be launched in these conditions, provided there are enough helpers, adequately clothed, but it is a tricky business.

Launching considerations

An ideal launching site would offer:

- reasonable access for vehicles and boats;
- off-site parking for vehicles and trailers;
- wide slipway;
- strong construction (if of timber, check that it will take the weight of your vehicle);
- not too steep an angle;
- clean (free from seaweed and slime, so a person can stand on it without slipping);
- sufficient water for launching and recovery at all states of the tide, or reasonable access;
- pontoons for mooring;
- a hard that will take the weight of vehicle and trailer wheels if the site is tidal and dries out;
- an electric winch or tractor to put in and out;
- fresh water available for washing down;
- changing facilities and toilets nearby;
- food available nearby;
- fuel in the vicinity;
- telephone;
- an area of water offering shelter from the open sea.

4

Weather

Make sure you obtain a weather forecast several hours before you go afloat on a large area of water. Small inland lakes and enclosed areas of estuary usually offer shelter and small boats are often manageable here as opposed to the open sea.

The most important factor, apart from the obvious – sun or rain – is the strength and direction of the wind, since this will determine the state of the water. Strong winds build large waves, while the direction of the wind determines the nature and effect of the waves.

For large vessels at sea, Beaufort Force 8 is recognised as a gale, but gale warnings for small ships in inshore waters are broadcast whenever the wind strength is expected to reach Force 5/6 (20 knots). Inexperienced boat handlers should not take their boats out in winds greater than Force 4. I refer to Force 6 as a dinghy sailor's gale.

Because Beaufort is measured at 33 ft (10m) above sea level (in clear air), it is impossible to gauge wind strength by simply standing on the seashore and testing the wind against your face. Use a hand-held wind gauge and make the necessary adjustments to your recorded wind strengths (the wind loses its strength by approximately one-third at sea level because of the drag effect of the waves).

Depending on whether the wind is travelling with the current or against it, the same strength of wind will have an entirely different effect on the state of the sea. For example, if a Force 4 wind is travelling with the current, the sea will be fairly choppy but the distance between wave crests will be stretched. If a Force 4 wind is blowing against the current, it will hold up the movement of the current and the waves will be closer together. Because the volume of water within the waves from crest to crest is the same, the waves heap upwards and will become very lumpy and even dangerous, (white crests and standing waves).

The direction of the wind relative to the coast is also important. A near-gale blowing off the land may have little effect on the immediate sea state, but the further one leaves the shelter of the shore, the more dangerous it can become. The same wind blowing in from the sea will build up big, dangerous waves.

Wind speeds

Beaufort force	General description	Speed (knots)
0	Calm	Under 1
1	Light	1–3
2	Light	4-6
3	Light	7–10
4	Moderate	11–16
5	Fresh	17–21
6	Strong	22–27
7	Strong	28–33
8	Gale	34-40
9	Severe gale	41–47
10	Storm	48–55
11	Violent storm	56–63
12	Hurricane	64 and over
		over

Speeds of weather systems
In the shipping forecast the speed of an approaching high- or low-pressure area is indicated by the following terminology:

Slowly	0–15 knots
Steadily	15–25 knots
Rather quickly	25–35 knots
Rapidly	35–45 knots
Very rapidly	Over 45 knots

Timing of gale warnings (at the time of the forecast)

Imminent	within 6 hours
Soon	6–12 hours
Later*	12–24 hours

* 'Later' is also used when referring to wind changes in forecasts.

4

The weather map

The weather maps used by forecasters are built up from measurements of atmospheric pressure: the weight of the air on the Earth's surface. This pressure changes as the air temperature changes: warm air will rise and create a low-pressure area, while cold air will sink and create a high-pressure area. As the warm air rises, it allows the cold, heavy air to rush in to balance out the pressure, and we experience this air movement as wind.

Gales occur when there is a large difference between the area of high pressure and the area of low pressure. The low-pressure area draws in the surrounding cold, heavy air at high velocity. Low-pressure areas are unstable with rain and wind, whereas high-pressure areas enjoy more stable conditions.

Sources of weather information

Information regarding the weather can be obtained from:

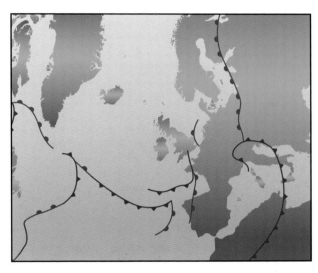

- local and national television (weather forecasts are given at set times);

- national radio (weather forecasts are given at set times – gale warnings are given as and when needed);

- marine weather services;

- VHF marine broadcasts;

- VHF marine radio (ship-ship and ship-shore);

- local radio in coastal areas;

- telephone pre-recorded services;

- coastguard stations;

- harbour masters;

- newspapers.

So there is no excuse for failing to be aware of the expected weather!

Remember that the wind direction and sea state can change within minutes, regardless of the forecast, so always keep an eye open for visual changes in the weather. When the wind increases and the sky begins to fill with very dark clouds, it is wise to be safe rather than sorry, and head for the shore.

5 Launching

Before you consider launching your boat, check the weather forecast. Then check the wind direction and the effect it is having on the water. If the wind is blowing from the water onto the land and creating large waves, launching will not only be very difficult but may also be dangerous. If the wind is coming across the land and blowing out to sea, the water will be quite flat. This is ideal for launching, but remember that the wind can change direction during the day. Conditions at 10 a.m. might be fine, but if a wind shift is predicted four hours later, it could make recovery very difficult by heaping up large breaking waves.

The other important area to check is the state of the tide. There are many tidal launching sites that dry out and can only be used for a few hours each side of high water. Marker posts indicating the height of water are generally situated close to the shore at such sites, and when the water level falls to a certain point all craft have to be removed from the water, otherwise they will run aground.

Ideal launching

Ideal conditions for launching would be no wind and no tide, and a slipway that allows the car to stay attached to the trailer throughout. The wheels of the car should not go anywhere near the water, and the wheel bearings on the trailer should remain above the surface. The angle of the slipway and the depth of the water should allow the craft to be slid off the trailer with a gentle push. This situation does not happen very often

Launching in the real world

It is not quite the same in the real world and one or two other considerations need to be taken on board.

Final preparations:

- Position the vehicle and boat out of the way of other users of the slipway.
- Remove the lighting board and electric cable from the trailer and place in the vehicle. Don't leave it on the ground and drive over it.
- Remove the boat ties and the protective cover from the engine and boat.

Prepare the craft:

- Complete the engine check, securing everything on board.
- Check fuel, oil (and water, if an inboard engine); four-stroke engines have an oil sump.
- Check the fuel system and ensure everything is ready to fire up.
- Check the hull for visible damage.

- Check the clothes of all crew and remember the lifejackets.
- Check the painter is attached to the bow. (This is the most important rope on small boats.)
- Check all drain bungs are in place.
- Keep the trailer winch cable, or strop, attached to the boat until the craft is in the water. If you take this off and then move down a steep slipway, the boat may slide off the trailer onto the ground, damaging the hull.
- One competent driver could be in the boat for the launch.
- Ensure the engine is tilted up on the hydraulics or, if manual, locked in the up position. If the engine is down when launching, serious damage could occur.

Do remember to remove all straps, propeller bags and lighting boards before launching.

The launch:

- Reverse the vehicle and boat towards the water, taking care not to submerge the wheels of the vehicle.
- When the boat starts to float at the stern, stop the vehicle and secure the brakes.
- Assuming the launch conditions are ideal, the driver onboard can lower the engine into the water, ensuring that it does not touch the bottom. The engine does not need to be completely down, as long as the cooling water intake is below the waterline.
- If you are the boat driver, follow the recommended start procedure and start the engine.

If you have a plug, make it secure. A small amount of grease before insertion helps the sealing.

- With an outboard immediately check that the cooling water is circulating through the engine. If not, close down the engine and refer to the section on 'Troubleshooting' in Chapter 12. (It normally takes a few seconds for the water to circulate. A few engines have thermostat control and take much longer.)

5

- Set the engine revolutions to around 1,500 rpm and allow a short time to warm up. If this is skimped, the engine is likely to stall when you engage gear, leaving the boat drifting around out of control.

- With the engine happily ticking over in neutral, ask to be released from the winch cable.

- Engage reverse gear and slowly go astern off the trailer. Pick up a mooring, anchor, or tie up to a jetty or pontoon – only if you have sufficient depth of water.

- The vehicle and trailer can now be removed from the slipway and parked safely above the high-water mark.

Remember the 5 P's: Pre-preparation prevents pretty poor performance.

DO NOT OBSTRUCT THE SLIPWAY – EMERGENCY VEHICLES MAY REQUIRE ACCESS AT ANY TIME

Wind and tide

Consideration has to be given to the variations in tide and wind and their combined effects. In practice, you should do all the final preparation as itemised above, and then pause. Look at the water. What is happening? Is the tide rising or falling? Is the wind stronger or weaker than the tide? Is the wind in the same direction as the tide, or against it? Look at other boats, especially those at anchor or on moorings. Look at flags or smoke to assess the wind direction. If the tide is stronger than the wind, the boats on moorings will point into the tide. These are described as 'tide rode'. If the wind is stronger than the tide and coming from a different direction, moored boats could be pointing at the wind or at a point between the direction of the wind and tide. These are referred to as 'wind rode'. Deep-keeled sailing boats will be more influenced by tide than shallow-drafted motorboats.

It is important to be able to discern which is stronger – the wind or the tide – because your boat will drift with wind or current immediately it is released from its trailer. You must ensure you have sufficient room to manoeuvre and allow for the drift before your boat starts to move under its own power. Once you have planned a course of action, carry on with the launch procedure.

Starting the engine

Outboard Four-stroke/Two-stroke

- Check the fuel. (Two-stroke oil?)
- Open the air vent on the fuel tank, (if necessary).
- Prime the engine by squeezing the bulb in the fuel line until you feel a resistance. (Make sure the bulb is fitted so that the arrow points down the line towards the engine.)
- Turn the choke control on, either manually (on a hand-pull engine) or by pushing the key, button or switch (electric start). Make sure the kill cord is fitted, or the engine will not (or should not) start, (unless automatic choke).
- Check that the gears are in neutral and open the override throttle, (if necessary).
- With an electric start, fire up the engine by using the starter. With a hand-pull engine, make sure you are balanced and clear of other crew members and give a good solid pull on the cord.
- The engine should have started by the third attempt. Immediately it fires, close the choke or switch it off.
- Adjust the throttle to roughly 1,500 rpm and check that the cooling water is circulating.
- Warm up the engine for three minutes.
- Check that both forward and reverse gears are working before moving off, (only if safe to do so).

Inboard

- Turn on the electricity at the isolation switch.
- Switch on the air blower for five minutes.
- Check that the fuel is on.
- Isolate the gear lever from the gears.
- Pump the gear/accelerator lever forward about three times to inject fuel into the carburettors, (if necessary).
- Set the lever in fast tick-over position.
- Start the engine by giving short bursts on the starter. If it fails to start after several attempts something could be wrong.
- Check that all the dials and controls are working, and that the cooling water is circulating.
- Warm up the engine for three minutes at the recommended warm-up speed.
- While at tick over, re-engage the gears and check forward and reverse before leaving the pontoon or mooring.

Electronic ignition and fuel-injected motors are not fitted with choke control.

- On all boats, check steering before leaving.
- Slow running – use airblower.

To stay in control after the boat is released from the trailer, go astern into the direction from which the wind or tide is coming. This will stop the boat being swept sideways – onto other craft, ashore or aground. Watch others and don't be tempted to copy their mistakes. Move out a long way into deep water before attempting to go ahead. Watch the stern swing and be careful not to drive the back of the boat over the trailer.

If the wind is really strong it can pile up big waves that may wash the boat straight off its trailer. Even larger waves will break right over the stern. If in any doubt, do not launch.

Launching from a hard in shallow water

Hards are simply hard areas of shingle, strong enough to take a heavy vehicle without it sinking in. This only applies to the centre of the hard, though, for the movement of water across shingle moves the stones off the centre to the edges, where they stick in the mud. The edges look hard but this is misleading and they should be avoided. Speak to the person in charge and seek their advice.

The slope of the hard is often variable, starting shallow and then falling away into deep water. Many hards can only be used at certain hours either side of high water.

Small lightweight boats only

At some launching hards the water is shallow for many metres before it becomes deep enough to launch a boat. If you follow the method given above, the water will come well over the door sills of your launch vehicle. One answer is to use a long rope. This has several advantages:

- It prevents the trailer disappearing after launching.

- It can be used to recover the trailer after launching, and to recover boat and trailer at the end of the day.

- It keeps the vehicle dry.

- It reduces the chance of physical injury if the risk is assessed correctly.

The technique of launching with the rope in shallow water is as follows:

- Having made all final checks, reverse down the hard and stop the tow vehicle clear of the waterline – remember tide rises and falls.

- Drop and secure the jockey wheel – keep trailer attached.

- Attach the end of the long rope to the trailer, using a bowline knot. Loop the rope around the ball hitch on the tow vehicle. This turn around the ball hitch will hold a small sportsboat. Keep the angle of the rope low down, otherwise it might come off the ball hitch.

- While holding the rope, release the trailer from the ball hitch. Be careful not to let your hand be crushed at the ball hitch as the trailer and boat slide into the water. Do not let the rope spin through your hand; rope burn is very painful.

- If the trailer has brakes, use the handbrake lever to control the trailer as it rolls down the slip into the water. Be aware that most trailer brake units do not hold very well on a slope. Meanwhile allow the rope to slip around the ball hitch on the tow vehicle.

- If there are no brakes on the trailer, use the rope to control the trailer as it rolls downhill. The ball hitch takes most of the strain so you should have no difficulty stopping the trailer, but take care not to release the rope or it may burn your hands.

- When the boat starts to float at the stern, secure the rope to the tow vehicle using a clove hitch.

- Wade out, release the boat from the winch cable/strop and gently push it off the trailer. Hold onto the painter and move the boat away from the trailer. The boat will swing round to point into the wind or tidal stream.

- Alternatively, if the water is deep enough and whilst the boat is on the trailer, lower the engine and start up. When all is ready, release the bow strop, jump back onboard and reverse off into deep water.

- Heavy boats require special considerations regarding safe launching and recovery.

- Meanwhile, someone else can retrieve the trailer by towing it out on the rope.

- When the car driver returns, he or she can climb aboard while the other crew member holds the bow of the boat in the shallow water.

- Use the paddles – NOT the engine – to move the boat into deeper water where you can pick up a mooring. Only use the engine if you are quite sure there is no danger of grounding the propeller.

Trailer still attached to rope by vehicle.

Drive the vehicle forward, pulling trailer out of the water.

Never allow the boat to drift while you try to start the engine. If it is reluctant to start you could easily drift half a mile or more before you get under control, and if you have a mechanical problem you could soon be in serious trouble. Trying to paddle a sportsboat against the wind and/or tide to return to the hard is virtually impossible. Having launched the boat, tie it to a nearby jetty or mooring before turning your attention to the engine. If there is nothing to tie it to, consider using the anchor.

Fixed-rope method

An alternative method is to position a large mooring out to sea with a rope running along the seabed and back to the shore. This rope is fixed to the shore above the high-water mark. You can use this rope to manhandle the boat out into deep water. This technique is safer and requires fewer people in the water.

When you return to the shore, pick up this mooring, switch off and lift the engine. Then, by using the rope, work your way back to the beach.

Experienced crews only

A crew of three can launch a boat into breaking waves, but it requires a rare determination. For this example, the craft is a rigid inflatable of around 13ft (4m).

- Move the boat off the trailer. Push or carry the boat out into the water bow first. One person is aboard and prepared to start the engine. The other two are holding the boat, one each side, and quickly moving it into deep water.

- The first breaking wave to strike the boat may ride over the bow and may begin to fill it up. Quickly move into the deeper water, lower the engine and fire up.

- By this time, the second and third waves will have broken into the boat, rapidly filling it with water and weighing it down.

- Quickly go into gear as the crew roll in, put the power on and drive into the next wave. The bow rises as the power comes on, causing the water to rush to the stern. Make sure it doesn't overwhelm the engine and swamp it. Drive through the next wave and into the clear water beyond the surf.

- Open up the transom flaps or elephant trunking and empty the craft. You may need to use a bucket or bailer to speed up the process. Depending on the type of self-bailer it could be open prior to launching.

Heavy boats require serious equipment for safe launching. Land Rover with a power winch.

6 Starting out

Before you start to carry out slow-speed handling in your boat you need to become familiar with the controls.

Steering
There are two basic types of steering:

1   Tiller steering, which is often found on boats with engines of up to 20hp.

2   A steering wheel, also known as the helm, which gives better control and a more comfortable driving position on boats fitted with engines of over 20hp.

Gear and acceleration
Sometimes very small outboard engines do not have a gearbox. Once started, they are in direct drive, so to go in a reverse direction you rotate the engine through 180°. Larger engines are fitted with one forward and one reverse gear. About the first 30° movement of the lever engages the gear either forward or reverse. As the gear shift lever is moved further forwards or backwards, acceleration will be increased. If you move the lever too slowly from neutral, the gear teeth will fail to engage cleanly, causing damage to the gearbox. You will hear a horrible grating sound. When changing gear, always return the lever to neutral and pause a while before changing gear. Fast boats with big engines will often have a foot throttle, which enables the helm to keep both hands on the wheel.

Tiller control, kill cord around wrist.

Helm layout for a fast cruiser.

Caution: Car drivers used to an automatic gear box sometimes move the gear lever the wrong way instinctively and go into astern instead of ahead.

Kill switch / kill cord
Most outboard engines and many inboard engines are now fitted with a kill switch (emergency stop switch, or lanyard). This is a cord that is clipped to the helmsman's wrist or leg or firmly to some part of their clothing. It is attached to a trip switch at the control box. In an emergency the cord is pulled from the switch, isolating power to the engine, (ignition circuit).

The advantages of this should be obvious. If the helmsman falls overboard the engine cuts out and the boat stops. Without the kill switch the boat could well disappear over the horizon leaving the helmsman helpless in the water. If the boat hits a steep wave at the wrong angle it could easily eject the whole crew into the water. On the open sea the consequences could be fatal if the kill switch is not being used. Having witnessed a man die at sea from a propeller, please use it.

Kill cord around the leg is best for helm position with wheel.

Fuel tanks

Many small sportsboats have portable fuel tanks, which need to be connected to the fuel line. Most outboard engines have to be primed with fuel before they will start. Priming the engine is the last thing that you do after you have lowered the engine into its down position. Large boats will have fitted fuel tanks. This enables greater distances to be covered without refilling or changing tanks whilst under way. Ensure all portable fuel tanks are secure and that the fuel lines and connectors are in good order. Large, new, 4-stroke engines seldom require priming.

Care with fuelling like this. No smoking, no splashing, no dirt, no rain – and fire extinguisher at the ready.

Pre-start checks

Cockpit check

Before moving away or even climbing on board:

- Take a visual all-round look at what is happening.
- Consider where the wind is coming from and how it will affect the boat.
- Consider the direction of the current.
- Take into consideration the amount and type of traffic on the water.

Propeller check

Prior to starting the engine ensure that it is in the down position and then carry out a propeller check looking for:

- depth of water;
- obstructions around the propeller;
- people around the propeller.

Every time the engine has been stopped make a rule to request a visual 'prop check' from the crew, or do it yourself.

With the propeller clear of obstructions, move to the helming position and start the engine, following the maker's recommended starting procedure. Once the engine is started, check for water circulation. With outboard engines this is a visible stream of water. (A few big outboards have a thermostat control and will not show a water telltale until a set worki ng temperature is reached. This may take several minutes.) With inboard engines you would normally watch the dials on the cockpit. Connect the 'kill cord'.

Check the direction for pulling away from your starting position. Check that it is clear to move away. Having slowly moved away using wind and current to the best advantage, check that:

- the crew are secure;
- fenders, if used, are removed and made secure;
- stern lines are removed from the stern of the boat;
- the painter or bow line is made secure amidships;
- all loose items are stowed and/or made secure.

Slow manoeuvring

Driving a boat is not like driving a car. For one thing you steer with the back rather than the front. This can be disconcerting at first, particularly when you are in a tight corner. Even more alarming is the effect of the wind and tide. A boat blown by the wind tends to slide sideways over a watery road, which itself is sliding to and fro over the ground. A combination of these two effects can be confusing, frustrating, expensive and sometimes dangerous; you must learn to allow for them and make use of them. The ability to use wind and tide constructively is one of the marks of a good boat handler.

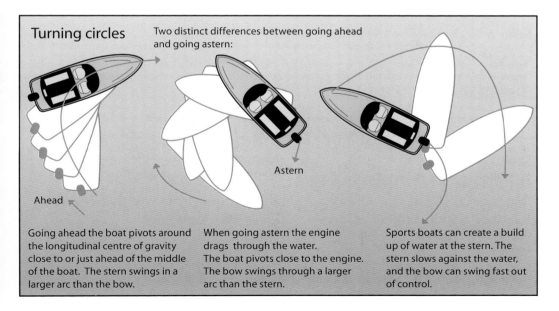

Turning circles

Two distinct differences between going ahead and going astern:

Astern

Ahead

Going ahead the boat pivots around the longitudinal centre of gravity close to or just ahead of the middle of the boat. The stern swings in a larger arc than the bow.

When going astern the engine drags through the water. The boat pivots close to the engine. The bow swings through a larger arc than the stern.

Sports boats can create a build up of water at the stern. The stern slows against the water, and the bow can swing fast out of control.

6

Gurgling speed or trolling

Gurgling speed is the speed of a vessel moving through the water whilst making the least possible amount of wave disturbance at the back of the boat. The bow hasn't raised and the stern hasn't dipped. The boat hasn't reached its displacement speed. It is the speed at which steerage can be controlled and where the vessel can move amongst moored vessels without causing a disturbance. Always look behind and check the size of the stern wave following you. Just because the water is flat in front doesn't mean all is well astern of you. The man up the mast of a yacht changing a light bulb will not too impressed when swung through an arc of 30°.

Gurgling or trolling   *Just above displacement speed, stern down – bow up*

Calculating displacement speed

I am always asked questions about slow speed and what 8 knots of speed actually looks and feels like. When a boat is travelling at its displacement speed it creates a bow wave and a stern wave with a suction area amidships. If the boat exceeds its displacement speed, the bow will lift and the stern will sink down.

Take the square root of the hull at waterline length in feet and multiply this root number by 1.32. (To make the mental arithmetic a little simpler, use the factor 1.4 instead of 1.32.)

Example:
Waterline length is 16 feet. Square root is 4.

Multiply 4 by 1.4 = 5.6.
This figure of 5.6 is the approximate displacement speed of this length of hull in knots.

For metric:
Convert the metres and tenths into feet and inches.
Multiply metres by 39.37 to convert to inches.
Divide by 12 to make feet.

The gurgling speed will be less – at around 3–4 knots

Current

In order to effectively master boat control it is necessary to appreciate the power of the tide or current. On a day when there is little or no wind, move your boat out into open water, switch off the power and sit. Study the drift. The current movement will change over a period of time. If there is no wind the boat will drift with the current. With the engine now running and in forward gear, face the boat into the current. Ensure that the approaching current is passing the bow exactly equally along both sides. When in position, drop the gear lever into neutral and use the current as the brake. The boat will gently slow down and stop over the ground. Once the boat has stopped over the ground, the water will still pass the hull at the speed of the current. Left in this position the boat will eventually stop and start to slowly drift backwards.

Keep the bow facing the current and, as soon as you notice the boat starting to drift backwards, engage forward gear (but only on tick over) until the boat starts once more to move forwards. Move gears into neutral, and again the boat will slow down and stop. Without any use of reverse gear the boat will stand still over the ground. The quicker the current moves, the more the power is required to hold station over the ground.

Under power the lower drive leg or outboard engine leg acts as the rudder to direct the stern. Many say that the power has to be applied before you have steerage. This is not true as the lower leg offers a little steerage all the time water is streaming past the hull. But in order to keep the bow facing the current it is necessary to adjust the position of the lower leg. If the bow starts to drift to port (left), spin the top of the wheel to the right. The water passing the leg will move the back of the boat to the left, bringing the bow back to face the current. If the hull is allowed to drift at the same speed as the current, any spinning of the wheel will be lost. As soon as the bow moves off its heading by a few degrees, power will have to be used to bring the bow back into the current.

Wind

One can have the boat perfectly balanced against the current and then suddenly be pushed off course by an unseen gust of wind. Wind direction can be seen by the way the flags fly on stationary boats, the direction smoke drifts from a bonfire or chimney and the direction that birds take flight. (Large birds such as swans take off into the wind.)

A further and often better method of discovering wind direction is to look at the waves. Wind-generated waves are usually at right angles to the direction of the wind. When the wind is approaching (looking to windward) the waves appear to have dark-coloured, sharp edges, whereas looking downwind (to leeward) the waves appear to have soft, sloping edges. Wind waves are generally at 90 degrees to the wind. This will accurately show wind direction, but what of strength and gusts? A gust of wind on the water can be seen as a dark patch moving fast across the surface. Just watch the surface on a windy day and the pattern on the water will give early warning of an extra-heavy gust. Some of the dark areas will pass by without effect, whereas others will build quickly and very close, catching one off guard. With a very steady breeze the water will be of a uniform pattern.Handling in wind and current

Never work to the wind alone. A flag will give you the wind direction but is not affected by the power of the current. When you are returning from a trip out, always come back in and drop into neutral. Watch carefully and decide on the direction of approach. Once you have found the position where the boat will stop, use this angle of approach to pick up your mooring or come alongside your jetty. When correctly balanced, you should not need to use reverse (unless you have chosen the stern approach).

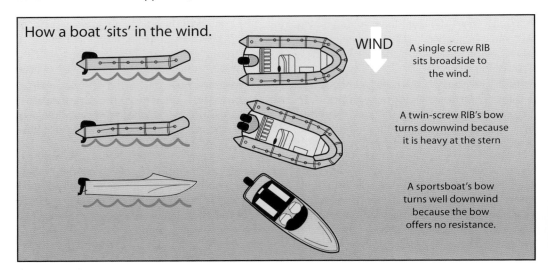

How a boat 'sits' in the wind.

WIND

A single screw RIB sits broadside to the wind.

A twin-screw RIB's bow turns downwind because it is heavy at the stern

A sportsboat's bow turns well downwind because the bow offers no resistance.

Ferry gliding

Ferry gliding, or stemming the tide, is an intricate part of boat manoeuvring at slow speeds. Move your boat into the tidal stream/current and hold position. To find out if you are stationary you will need to look at other craft on moorings, jetties, the foreshore, trees and buildings and use these as transit marks. If you are fortunate to have a river or estuary in a quiet and empty backwater, it may be necessary to drop a couple of sinkers (floating buoys). Place them fairly close together across the current and use them as transits. Having mastered holding station over the ground, deliberately turn the top of the helm wheel in the direction you wish to go. The stern should start to respond in the current. As the bow turns slightly off the direct line of the current to around 10–15° to the helm, and as the boat starts to drift astern, just drop the lever into ahead tick over. The boat will now move across at the angle you have chosen. As soon as forward movement becomes apparent, drop the gears back into neutral. The boat will now be moving sideways. As long as it does not go too much astern or ahead it will move sideways between two points.

This an important exercise for mooring against a jetty, as the current acts as the brake. Once ferry gliding has been mastered going ahead, turn the boat around, offer the stern to the current and hold station. As the boat starts to swing in the current, move the top of the helm wheel in the direction that you wish to go in order to correct the drift. Usually the stern tick over gives sufficient power. Having engaged reverse there will be a short delay before the boat starts moving. Be patient. If you have the engine facing the correct direction, the hull will start to move back into a central position in line with the water current. A sideways stern approach to a jetty offers an amazingly high degree of accuracy. In some conditions, it is the only option available for a satisfactory docking.

The principle explained
The boat stands still over the ground with the water streaming past both sides. As soon as the boat turns to port or starboard there is an increase of pressure down the side facing the current. This causes the boat to crab sideways into the low-pressure area created on the opposite side. Using this ferry glide principle, I was able to stand still under the bridges on the Thames each time a heavy shower came through. This kept me dry whilst others around me were getting very wet.

If there is sufficient current you could use the ferry glide principle to move sideways across the water to the mooring. A choice can also be made as to whether to pick up forwards or astern. If using the astern approach onto a mooring, always check that the mooring is clean – without floating lines etc. You can approach a swinging mooring from any direction. This is not the case with a jetty, which is fixed. When docking against a jetty, again check the direction of wind and current. Never assume that the boats already on the jetty are facing the correct way. They could have arrived some hours earlier when tide and wind were in a totally different direction.

Holding station over the ground and using the ferry glide technique is superb when you are approaching a busy jetty. If a boat is about to leave and is making space for you, just stand still

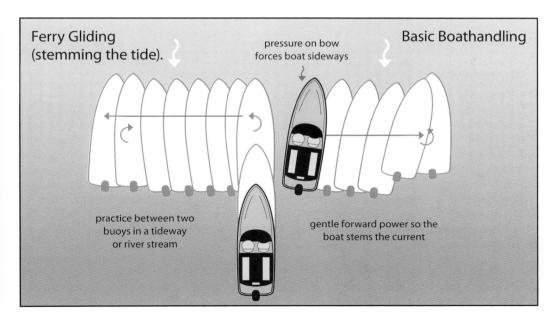

Ferry Gliding (stemming the tide).

pressure on bow forces boat sideways

Basic Boathandling

practice between two buoys in a tideway or river stream

gentle forward power so the boat stems the current

over the ground and block anyone else's approach to this space. This manoeuvre is no different to waiting for someone to leave a car parking space. If you were to drive off round the car park, it is likely that by the time you reached the spot again it would have been filled by another vehicle. A helm who does not understand the basic principles of holding a boat stationary in the wind and current will cruise around in a long circle only to find the space has been taken by others.

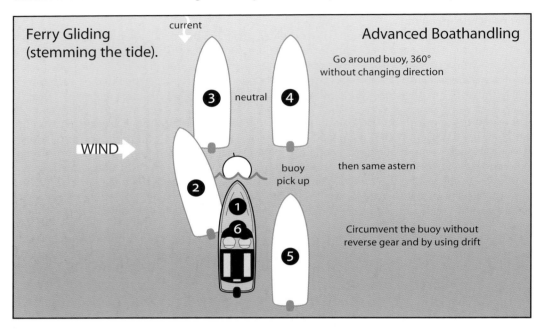

Figures of eight

Driving around a couple of buoys or moored boats at gurgling speed is an excellent way to learn about your boat. Choose two marks about six or eight boat lengths apart and weave your way around them in forward gear. Notice the way the stern kicks out when you turn. Any object alongside you in the water needs to be avoided, so turn the wheel at it when moving forward. This will result in the back of the boat moving away from the object. The figure-of-eight course around the buoys emphasises this point. You will have to watch for the effects of wind and tide. You will probably have to compensate for a cross tide or crosswind, which will drive the boat to one side, while a tide that is flowing with or against you will change the rate at which the boat reacts to the helm. As you circle the two buoys try to imagine a piece of rope attached to you and to the top of the buoy. Keep the imaginary rope taut. This is not an easy exercise. The buoy is anchored to the ground and the water and air are moving.

Keep going until you can steer a steady course around the marks. Now try the same route in reverse. When you are travelling astern there will be no problem travelling with the wind. However, as the stern of the boat turns to face the wind, the waves will start to break over the back of the boat.

Do take care that you don't move too quickly astern into waves. With large engines and boats fitted with bathing platforms, it is possible to put on so much power going astern that the boat will actually go under water and swamp.

Whilst going forward around the two buoys, try to establish the pivot point of your boat. When going astern you will note that the pivot point is different than when going ahead. Find out exactly where your turning circles are. If you turn at the buoy when going astern, the boat will hit it. This is the opposite swing to going ahead.

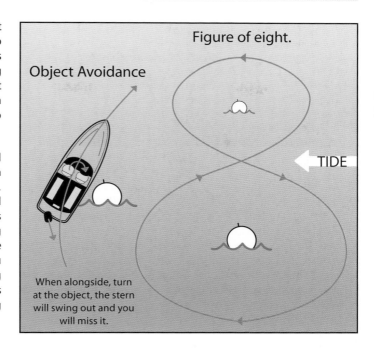

Figure of eight.

Object Avoidance

TIDE

When alongside, turn at the object, the stern will swing out and you will miss it.

Twin engines

The above can be completed using both drive units together. However, you can also complete the turns using one engine ahead and one astern. Using one engine ahead on tick over, adjust the forward movement by continually adjusting astern thrust on the other engine.

Three-point turn (single engine)

In a harbour, marina or close to moored boats you may find yourself in a position where you cannot turn around in one movement. The only option is a manoeuvre

When going astern – look astern!

similar to that of a car turning around in a narrow road. Usually called a three-point turn, this manoeuvre may involve several forward and reverse alterations, but it can be greatly simplified by creative use of the wind and tide. It is well worth practising the following:

- Study the area in which you have to turn. Ensure that you have room for the back of your boat to swing – remember that it swings outwards on the turn. Check the wind and tide and slowly start the forward turn on a hard lock in tick over into the wind and/or tide. In a narrow lane do not turn more than 90°across the lane.

6

Sufficient power and speed to maintain control, especially with wind and current

■ As the boat moves to this 90° position, drop into neutral. Allow the boat to drift forwards because you need all the room astern to complete the turn. Quickly spin the helm in the other direction. Engage reverse gear on tick over. Check the area astern is clear and watch the water that you are about to use. Move the boat back through a 45° angle to the original 90°. Go into neutral, spin the wheel to the opposite lock, moving the lever into forward drive on tick over. As the boat starts to move forward the back will swing. You should end up around centre to the channel and facing the opposite direction, having turned through 180°. Concentrate on your pivot points, use only sufficient power to move the boat and always try to be in neutral when you turn the wheel.

If it is very windy it is possible to use the wind to carry out the turn. First turn the bow through the wind and drop into neutral; this removes your forward movement but allows the boat to continue the turn. The wind on one side of the bow will continue to turn the boat in a confined area, and it is quite possible to turn the boat through 180° with just that small amount of forward movement into the first 90°.

In a strong wind the boat will have a tendency to drift sideways, so if you need to turn a long boat around in a very confined space you may be unable to turn the bow into the wind. The boat will simply drift sideways. If you have this problem, prepare the turn from an upwind position and turn the bow away from the wind in forward gear. In other words the bow is blown downwind. Then reverse back into the wind. Into neutral, swing hard to the other lock and engage forward gear to motor out in the opposite direction. Practise in a large area with plenty of room.

Bow through the wind, no power – drift into new position.

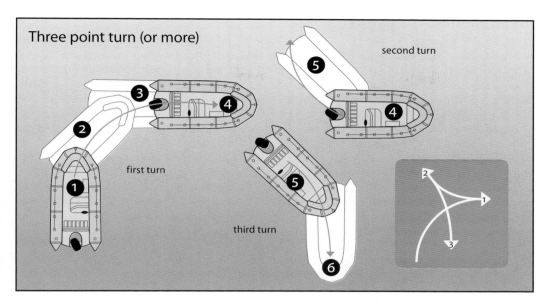

Three point turn (or more)

second turn

first turn

third turn

6

Be aware that it is very possible to get the boat out of position and straddled across other boats or jetties. You may not be able to engage gears.

Good seamanship may require you to organise your crew to fend off and push you around or to use ropes to complete the turn.

Practise these 180°turns in open water before trying them in a tight spot where you might hit something. A full 360° turn is also worth practising since it involves both the techniques described. Always ensure that you have room for the stern to swing. Check the stern and, if necessary, straighten the helm to avoid stern contact. Never ever go for power to move out of a tight spot.

Three-point turns (twin engines)

Boats with twin engines can be turned in just the same way, but by using one engine in forward gear and one in reverse you can rotate the boat in its own length without moving the steering helm. One ahead and one astern with outboard engines works very well. First have the steering wheel centralised. Depending on which way you wish to turn, engage the forward drive on the outside engine of the turn. Leave this throttle in tick over. Engage reverse on the inside engine. Because the propellers are designed to thrust forwards the engine on tick over going ahead will give forward movement as well as the turn. It is, therefore, necessary to increase the revs on the engine in astern gear to compensate for the forward movement. Obviously the engine going astern will be running faster than the engine going ahead. This is why I suggested leaving one engaged in forwards alone and making all your speed adjustments on the engine going astern. If you continually check that you are not moving forwards, the boat will rotate through 180° without actually using the area of water ahead or astern of it. The neutral throttle position is often used in this manoeuvre. If you become confused – stop moving. Never hit the power to move out of a problem as it could become very expensive.

It is possible to start from an alongside docking position in a marina, reverse out, rotate the boat around and move into a completely different channel, docking the boat without touching the steering wheel. Wind and current will have to be taken into consideration and used to advantage. This manoeuvre can be difficult if the engines are mounted very close together. And in answer to some critics, outboard engines can be used very successfully in rotating a boat through 180° or more.

Once the principles of twin-engine handling have been mastered you will find that manoeuvring with a twin-engine boat is much simple than when using a single screw.

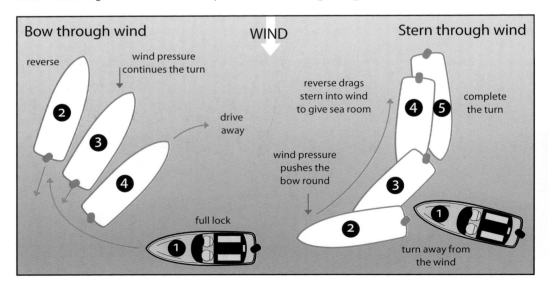

7 Very small boats

Small engines have integral fuel tanks and most do not have a gearbox. Once they have been started the propeller is immediately turning and they are off and away. If you want to go astern you twiddle the engine all the way around so that the propeller, which is still being turned by the engine, pushes the boat backwards.

Honda has developed a 2hp outboard engine with a slipping clutch. In other words, on tick over the propeller does not drive, but as soon as you accelerate, the propeller engages and gives you drive. This is an excellent improvement.

Where do I sit?

On a small boat with an outboard engine, tiller control and gears, the tiller control lever is usually on the left-hand side. A question often asked is, "which side do I sit?" Sit in a small boat in the best way possible, without upsetting the boat. If you are large, like me, once on board and seated within the boat you become very much a fixture. If I sit on the right-hand side of the boat and change gear, I turn my body towards the engine, place my right hand on the tiller control and use my left hand to change the gears. From this right-hand side of the boat I can still look ahead in the direction I am travelling. I can also maintain better control of the tiller from this position. I do not have to move my weight. I would probably be sitting in the boat and therefore more secure. Find the most comfortable place to sit and at the same time maintain control of the boat.

When starting the engine use the pull cord to turn the engine over. You need to be in a position to stop the engine and release the lock catch lever. Under the engine you will probably find a locking lever. This lever, in a locked position, prevents the engine from riding up out of the water when the reverse gear is engaged (if it has a reverse). It is useful to release this lever if you are working through shallow water, as it allows the engine to ride up out of the water if the skeg strikes the bottom. The lever must be unlocked when you are arriving on a beach otherwise damage will be caused to the engine/propeller. Your seated and secure position is, therefore, very important.

The larger outboard engines with tiller controls have a remote fuel tank connected to the engine with a fuel line. On the tiller you will find the accelerator twist grip and possibly the lanyard and stop button. On one side of the engine you may find the gear lever. On more modern engines the gear shift is mounted at the front, above the tiller control – a much better idea. Use the choke control for starting from cold. Usually there is a kill cord and/or stop button.

Boat trim and balance

Correct loading of a small boat is critical to the satisfaction of the journey you are about to make. Ensure equal distribution of people and cargo so that the boat is as level as possible. Once seated and under way be sure that no members of the crew move around. Large dogs in small boats have been the cause of a number of accidents. As the boat arrives at the jetty, the dog is the first to try and climb out, which may create a capsize alongside the jetty.

I once watched three well-built professional fishermen climb into a small tender. As it rocked back and forth each tried to balance the roll. Every individual effort was counter productive and, much to my amusement, the boat inverted. The water was just deep enough to cover their waders. Whilst standing in the water all three lifted the boat and emptied it out. The air was blue, their day was ruined and I have a wonderful picture in my mind of the three, squelching up the road to their van.

Handling a rubber boat

Controlling a small, flat-bottomed rubber tender with a little outboard engine is an art. Because they are flat bottomed they slide across the water, so it is important to drift them into turns. They handle in a similar way to a hovercraft, but as very few people have driven hovercraft, I will explain the technique to use.

Moving ahead in a straight line with a reasonable amount of power applied, push the tiller across for either a turn to port or starboard. Although the back of the boat turns, the boat will continue in the direction it was first travelling, sliding across the water sideways. Flat-bottomed rubber boats are like that – 'difficult'. When the boat is pointing in the direction you want to travel, straighten the helm. Continue to apply the same amount of power. The boat will eventually start travelling in a straight line in the direction that you are pointing.

It is important, therefore, when manoeuvring in a marina, to commence the turn from one bay to the next very early, in order to have the boat facing the right direction into the bay where you wish to travel. If you leave the turn too late the boat will slide into jetties and other boats – very entertaining to watch! It takes a little while to get used to it, but, once mastered, the technique is simple to use. On coming alongside a jetty or pontoon, approach at an angle of approximately 80°. Push the helm over so that you start to slide sideways, but still in the direction of the jetty, and reduce power. The boat should gently strike the jetty broadside, thus avoiding any possible bow damage. The helm sitting at the stern controlling the engine can now grab hold of the jetty without having to move about the boat.

You can twiddle the boat around a full 360°, as its turning circle, or pivot point, is totally different to that of any other boat you are likely to use. I suppose a bumper car at a funfair is similar.

Always ensure that the tubes of rubber boats are fully inflated. If they have an inflatable floor make sure that this is correctly fitted and correctly inflated. If you are very heavy and the boat is not inflated properly, it will fold up around you as you step in – and you will get that sinking feeling that all is not well.

If you are still having difficulty in steering, you are probably applying too much thought to the problem. Give the controls to a ten-year old, or even younger, and in no time at all, they will usually have cracked the problem! Naturally, if trying this approach, ensure you are on board at all times, supervising.

Putting the outboard engine on

If the boat can be assembled on dry land and then carried into the water complete, this is to be recommended. If you are launching a boat off a fairly high pontoon or from the back of a yacht, it may be advisable to place the boat into the water first and then hand the engine down to the crew member who has already climbed into the boat. Even small outboard engines are difficult to handle and are quite heavy. Tie a lanyard around the engine between the saddle bracket (the clamping screws), and hold this lanyard as you pass the engine down to your colleague in the boat. This lanyard will go some way to prevent the engine from dropping down in the water if you were to slip.

After the engine is attached and made secure, use a lanyard to tie the engine to the boat.

Think everything through thoroughly before starting out. I once watched a crew member, balancing in a tender, who found the engine too heavy to counterbalance with his body weight as he stood over the transom bracket. You can finish the tale yourself!

8 Mooring

To practise picking up a mooring, find a suitable empty mooring, one with sufficient room to manoeuvre. Also check whether it has long lines dangling from it just under the surface, as the last thing you want is the propeller caught in a rope.

You should aim to approach the mooring in a controlled manner and pick it up easily without using reverse gear. To do this, you have to be aware of:

- wind direction and strength;
- current direction and strength;
- wind and current direction combined.

You also need to consider:

- weight of boat;
- speed of boat;
- available room to manoeuvre,
- sufficient depth of water around the buoy.

To determine the wind direction look at rising smoke, flags, the direction of the waves and ripples. Waves are created by the wind and if they are undisturbed by other craft they will usually be at 90° to the wind.

To find the direction of the current, look at the mooring buoy itself. Which way is it leaning? Watch for the swirl of water around posts and jetties; the wave pattern around the obstacle will show you the water direction. If the water is clear, look at the direction the seaweed is pointing.

In practice the combined effect of wind and current will be indicated by the position of other craft on their moorings. Remember that a shallow-drafted sportsboat will be less influenced by the current than a deep-keeled yacht, and more affected by the wind. Always plan an escape route in case you have misjudged the conditions.

Tips

1   Slowly approach the mooring buoy from downwind – down tide – in a straight line. Gradually reduce speed until there is only a short distance between the boat and the mooring. Always reduce speed early. Most helms keep the power on for far too long. If you are slightly short of the mooring buoy you can always nudge ahead with a little power. The approach should be slightly off centre so that the pickup can be done on the starboard side of a traditional sportsboat. If the steering helm is on the left-hand side, I would recommend that the pickup is done on port side. With rigid inflatables and centre consoles the choice is yours.

2   Put the engine into neutral and let the weight of the boat carry you forward. This is referred to as carrying way. If your judgement is accurate, you will stop with the buoy alongside. With most small sportsboats, it is easier to pick the mooring up from alongside. This avoids someone having to climb over the windscreen and sit precariously on the bow. If you are travelling through the water too fast, you could ride straight over the top of the buoy. Engaging reverse gear could help to stop you in time but it's messy. Practise until you are able to stop by the buoy without using reverse. Most mooring buoys have a small pickup buoy in the water adjacent to the larger buoy. The pickup buoy often has a handle attached to it. Do not tie up to this handle; it is only intended to aid picking up by hand or boathook.

3   Pick up the mooring buoy. Use the painter to secure the boat to the chain, rope or steel ring with a round turn and two half hitches or a bowline finished with a half hitch.

Slowly approach. Grab the 'pick up buoy'. Tie to the chain or main buoy.

Leaving the mooring

1   First start the engine, but only after you have carried out the pre-start checks (see page 8). Check around you to ensure that there are no other craft hindering your departure.

2   Check the engine's direction and engage forward gear on tick over. Use just enough power to bring you alongside the mooring. When alongside, use your hand or boathook to pick up your painter. If it is clear to leave, cast off from the mooring buoy and secure the painter.

3   Allow the wind or tide to drift you off the mooring. When you are clear, move slowly ahead. As you turn remember that the directional thrust of the propeller will kick the stern out. Be careful not to propel the stern in the direction of the mooring and ride over it. (Remember – if you wish to avoid anything lying alongside the hull, turn the wheel at the object and the stern of the boat will miss it. This only works in forward gear.)

If you have snared a rope attached to the buoy, do not cut it free until you have made your boat secure to this buoy with other lines. At least whilst you are trapped you are secure.

8

Docking

Coming alongside a moored boat

Once you have mastered picking up a mooring buoy, coming alongside a moored boat is easy. Just follow the same method. Select your side of approach and prepare the painter and fenders. (I often use fenders in an inflatable boat, as replacing fenders is less expensive than replacing tubes.) You are now ready to make a slow, controlled approach. The moored boat you are approaching will probably be swinging around on the end of its rope. Stand back a little, judge the swing and then make the final approach. Try to carry out the approach at around 15° to 20° of angle to the boat. This is a better approach direction than trying to come from directly behind it. Once alongside the boat, pass your painter through a fairlead (if fitted) and/or tie it to a strong point such as a cleat. Remember to tie the stern using a breast rope.

Coming alongside a jetty or pontoon

The procedure for coming alongside a jetty is much the same, but you have to take account of the fact that a jetty or pontoon is a more or less immovable object attached to the land.

1 Establish a direction of approach, in a straight line and, if possible, against the wind and/or tide. Put out fenders, if necessary, and prepare your bow and stern lines. When approaching into the tide, the ferry glide procedure can be adopted. Where there is no wind and no tide, always try to approach at approximately an 15–20° angle to the jetty. When approaching directly parallel to the jetty, you will invariably end up with the shoulder of the boat striking the corner of the jetty. It is very difficult to accurately run parallel to a jetty. It is far better to make an angled approach.

2 Slowly move forward towards the jetty. Into neutral and judge speed. If the approach is too slow, you can always add a little more power. Allow the wind or tide to act as the brake to your forward motion.

20° angle of approach with just enough headway

Keep this angle until very close. Engine into neutral, drift towards jetty. Prior to striking jetty (next).

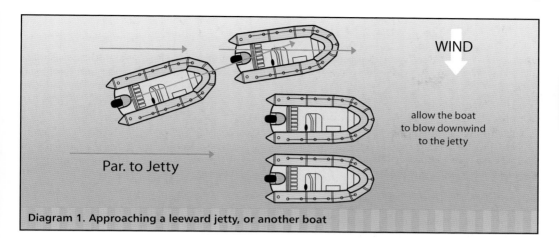

WIND

allow the boat
to blow downwind
to the jetty

Par. to Jetty

8

Diagram 1. Approaching a leeward jetty, or another boat

3   You should glide to a stop alongside. Take the prepared bow and stern lines, step ashore and secure them to a cleat, using a figure-of-eight lashing or, if to a bollard, a bowline or a clove hitch.

If wind and tide prevent a straight line of approach try the following:

With wind blowing onto the pontoon, jetty to leeward.

1   Approach slowly some metres away from the pontoon but parallel to it. Into neutral and allow the boat to come to rest. The wind will start to blow the boat sideways onto the pontoon. If the characteristic of the boat is for the bow to swing downwind, you will have to play the bow into the wind, keeping the stern towards the jetty until the last few metres of approach.

2   By adjusting the direction of the helm and by using forward or reverse in tick over, the boat will slide gently sideways onto the jetty.

Into astern, tick over and spin the helm at the jetty.

Forward movement will cease and the stern will swing towards the jetty. Power off when stationary – "tie up".

Further examples

Balance the boat and drift sideways onto the jetty — jetty to leeward.

Remember to organise mooring lines, otherwise the boat will drift away — jetty to windward.

Wind blowing off the jetty

Where the wind is blowing from the jetty, the effect is to blow the bow outwards and the whole boat away from the jetty.

1   Approach with sufficient power to maintain headway at an angle of approximately 15–20°. You must keep forward movement and, without turning the bow into the jetty, come into neutral.

2   Allow the weight of the boat to carry forwards towards the jetty. Before striking the jetty, engage reverse gear. As reverse gear is engaged, spin the steering wheel quickly towards the jetty. This will arrest your forward movement and, at the same time, pull the stern into the jetty.

Going astern alongside a jetty to windward

Fenders must be used. Do not spin the wheel at the jetty before engaging reverse gear otherwise the bow will swing into the jetty and hit it fairly hard. Hold the reverse gear just long enough to remove the forward movement. Once the boat is stationary, into neutral, step ashore and secure the craft. When stepping ashore do take the ropes with you. And please take ropes that are attached to the boat!

8

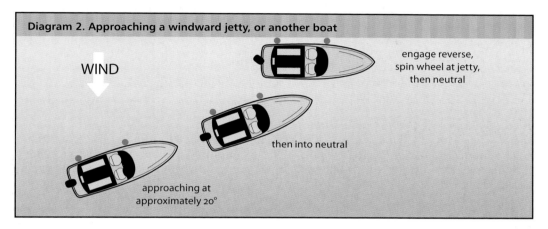

Astern docking, or down tide or downwind approach

Try doing the whole exercise going astern. I expect that you will find this more controllable than attempting the manoeuvre ahead. It is slower and becomes a much more gentle docking. The escape route is in place for the whole of the manoeuvre.

Drive down parallel to the jetty with the wind and/or current from behind you. Before you reach the parallel position to the jetty drop into neutral and allow the boat to drift. With the boat several metres out from the jetty, drop the lever into reverse tick over and wait for the forward movement to come off the boat. It will take a little while before the boat stops and starts to go astern. As it starts to slowly go astern, angle the engine into the jetty and you should discover a very accurate stern approach onto the jetty. In gear – out and in – nudge astern.

Mooring astern against wind and current

Marinas

Contact the marina before you arrive by phone or VHF. Most UK marinas listen out on Channel 80 or 37 (M). Ask permission to enter; the marina will give directions. On the approach, check the wind direction and watch for moving boats.

Astern docking in narrow marinas

Position the boat with the bow facing outwards and the stern facing the jetty. You should be several metres away from the jetty to give yourself time to get the boat under control and balanced when going astern.

Birdham Pool, Chichester – one of the oldest marina's in Britain.

Keeping approximately an 80° angle of approach to the jetty and before striking the jetty, turn the engine into the wind and/or current. As the stern starts to swing, the bow will gently arc around to come parallel to the jetty. If the timing is correct you can leave the helm hard over and apply just enough forward power to stop the backward movement and tuck the stern into the jetty.

Astern docking in very strong winds

The approach is similar to the above. The stern will hold stationary into the wind. Balance can be maintained by the use of a minimal amount of power. Slowly approach stern to the jetty. Have lines on the stern already prepared. When a stern quarter is close enough for a crew member to step ashore, walk off the transom onto the jetty and make one line secure to a cleat. The boat will now hang off this single line. When secure, spin the wheel at the jetty and gently apply forward power. The boat will pivot on its line, the bow will come around slowly and the boat will lay alongside the jetty.

Stern approach between two posts. Manhandle it in. Unlikely to be able to drive through gap. Keep fingers and legs well clear.

Note: In marinas you will always have control if you take the stern of your boat into the wind. In this position you can hold station very nearly indefinitely. Be patient. As long as the boat is drifting in the right direction, let it drift. Why upset it? Attempting the same manoeuvre with the bow into the wind is nearly impossible; as soon as way is lost the bow will be blown off course and the boat will spin around. Any use of forward power is often a disaster. The escape route will now be astern into the wind so why not start that way in the first place? Remember that good boat handling goes unnoticed. It is only the glorious foul ups that are remembered and talked about in the bar.

If the weather is too windy for a safe docking in a tight pontoon bay, use the outside visitors' jetty to drop off your crew with instructions to position themselves on the pontoon and on the boats around your slot to act as catchers. They are likely to be more use out of the boat than in it. Boathooks are useful and do prepare all lines and fenders before moving off.

If conditions are really serious, leave the boat safe on the visitors' jetty and move it later when the wind has abated. Good seamanship is just that – good seamanship. It doesn't mean one can do anything and put a boat anywhere in any condition. Seamanship is the making of seamanlike decisions, i.e. safe practice.

8

Rafting up
It is more than probable on a busy day that all side-to moorings are taken. The marina or harbour master may well ask you to raft up. Before coming alongside another boat certain checks need to be made. Stand off and ask permission from the crew on board to come alongside. By standing off it gives the crew on board the boat you wish to come alongside the time to prepare fenders to protect their boat from you. Standing off also gives you time to assess the wind and current direction and to set your fenders and lines. Once again, you need a controlled approach with a minimum amount of power. Once alongside secure lines. If you have not already found out how long the boat is going to be there, now is the time to ask. Technically you cannot secure to the boat that you have just come alongside. All your lines should go to the pontoon ashore. If you are three or four boats out you will need very long lengths of rope. Once you are secure, ask the crew that you are alongside if they are happy with your rope arrangements.

If you are alongside a yacht and wish to make your way to the pontoon, always go over the front of the yacht, never through the cockpit, unless requested to do so by the people on board. Please ensure that you are wearing soft shoes or deck shoes. Black hobnail boots are not welcome and you may end up 'keelhauled'. If you are using a small sportsboat and have arrived at the jetty first, you

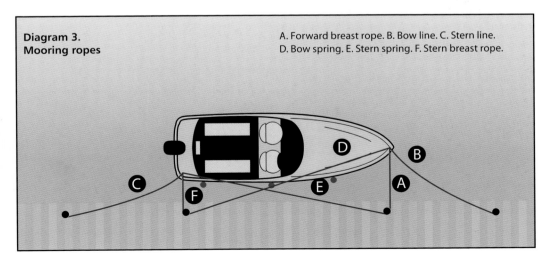

Diagram 3.
Mooring ropes

A. Forward breast rope. B. Bow line. C. Stern line.
D. Bow spring. E. Stern spring. F. Stern breast rope.

certainly would not wish to have a 50ft (15m) yacht on your outside, squashing you. Drop back or move away from the jetty and allow the bigger boat to moor up, and then come up alongside and tie on. Sportsboats are not a very common sight rafted up but it is possible for six to eight sportsboats to lie alongside each other on one small section of pontoon if it is done correctly. At least three fenders down each side are required, plus a bow line and a stern line to the pontoon or shore. Finish off with springs. Springs leading fore and aft are essential in preventing the rafting from rolling around the end of the jetty and striking other craft.

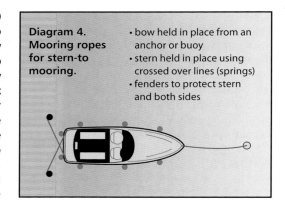

Diagram 4. Mooring ropes for stern-to mooring.
- bow held in place from an anchor or buoy
- stern held in place using crossed over lines (springs)
- fenders to protect stern and both sides

Turning the boat at the jetty, no engine – wind assisted
Bow attached

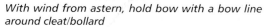

With wind from astern, hold bow with a bow line around cleat/bollard

Push stern out into the wind – the rest is history

Stern attached, no engine – wind assisted

With wind from the bow, attach the stern and push out the bow.

With use of ropes, one can ensure the boarding platform misses the jetty

Leaving a jetty

In the absence of wind or tide, take off the lines, push out the bow and motor slowly away with the helm straight! (Diagram 5.) If the wind and/or tide are along the jetty, always leave against the most powerful force. This gives a slow exit, under control and using the external forces to lever you away from the jetty.

8

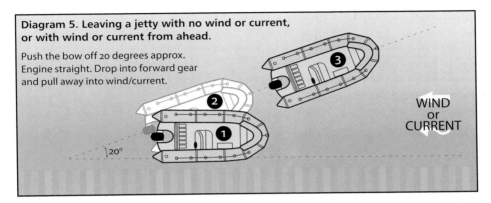

Diagram 5. Leaving a jetty with no wind or current, or with wind or current from ahead.

Push the bow off 20 degrees approx.
Engine straight. Drop into forward gear and pull away into wind/current.

WIND
or
CURRENT

20°

You are having a laugh! One cannot hold a boat as if walking a dog

Fix the line or take a turn around a cleat or bollard for strength and proper control

If one is attached at the stern, nudge forward/ahead, using rope as a spring

Bow will turn into jetty – make secure

Leaving if the wind is blowing you onto the jetty.
Use the bow spring or the stern spring, depending on the tide. If the tide is under your stern, take off all the ropes except the bow spring (rigged so you can slip it). Put some fenders at the bow, turn the wheel towards the jetty and motor slowly ahead (Diagram 6). The boat's stern will swing out. Finally, motor astern, retrieving the bowspring.

This method works well in any wind direction.

Leaving a jetty using a spring
A spring is useful if the tide is under your bow, or you want to go forwards.

1   From the stern, pass a rope around a bollard or cleat further ahead of your boat. Hold the end of this rope in your hand.

2   Release all other lines.

3   Put the helm over towards the jetty and engage reverse gear on tickover. Watch the bow.

4   Watch that you do not reverse into the boat behind you.

5   Leverage will pull the bow out. Now go into neutral, release your spring, straighten your helm and drive ahead.

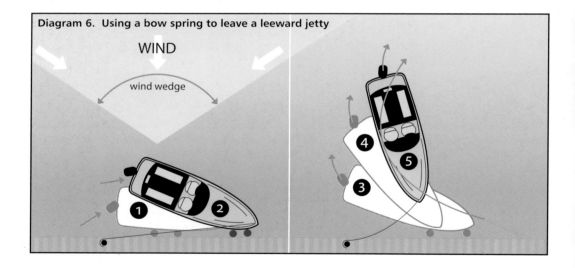

Diagram 6. Using a bow spring to leave a leeward jetty

WIND

wind wedge

Slip Line

A slip line is very useful when leaving. Cleat one end of the line, then pass it around the cleat or bollard on the dock. Finally bring it back to the boat and cleat it off. When you want to leave, release one end of the line and you can pull it off the bollard without leaving the boat. (Keep the rope clear of the propeller.)

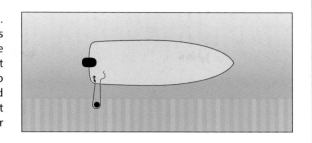

8

Leaving the boat on a pontoon

If you intend to leave your boat on a pontoon for some time it needs to be secured in such a way that it could withstand a gale. This will require a forward breast rope, a stern breast rope, one bow spring, one stern spring and, if you have room, one stern line and one bow line. Once you have all the lines in place, with the fenders set at the correct height, physically push the boat in all the different directions to ensure that the lines are correctly set and that the boat is not going to ram the end of the jetty or be rammed into another yacht or powerboat in a gale. Tie everything down and make secure. All ropes should be of good quality. Always leave the boat in preparation for a gale. It is now safe to go home and sleep peacefully.

Fenders all set at correct height and secure

Correctly moored alongside (two springs attached amidships)

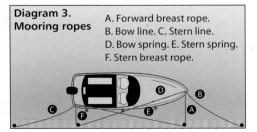

Diagram 3. Mooring ropes
A. Forward breast rope.
B. Bow line. C. Stern line.
D. Bow spring. E. Stern spring.
F. Stern breast rope.

9 Life begins at 25 (knots)

Before we look at high speeds across the water it is wise to try and understand how a hull flies.

Balance and trim

Trim on small boats is altered by the fore and aft position of crew and cargo. If there is too much weight at the front of the boat the bow will dig into the water. If there is too much weight at the back the boat will ride with the stern low and be difficult, if not impossible, to bring up onto the plane. Ideal trim varies from boat to boat. If you concentrate the weight at the centre you will not go far wrong to start with.

Balance

The boat's balance can easily be altered by 'side to side' weight distribution. If the boat is level all will be well. With two people in the boat the balance is usually fine, but a 252lb (114kg) driver sitting on one side of the boat will create an irregular hull contact with the water, causing speed and handling to suffer considerably. Since there should always be two people in a sportsboat this situation should never arise, but with three or more people you may have to give some thought to seating arrangements.

Trim

Small outboard engines on sportsboats are often manually lowered and raised. When in the lowered position they rest on an adjustable bar. This bar can be set according to the type of boat and its loading. Any setting is, therefore, a compromise, as it cannot be changed when under way.

Hydraulic trim

When pulling away for a straight run up onto the plane, the engine needs to be trimmed down. This is sometimes referred to as trimmed in, or leg trimmed in. If the engine is very close to the transom the back of the boat lifts up and forces the bow down when power is applied. By lifting the back of the boat it comes up onto the plane very quickly but leaves the boat with the bow dug in. As soon as the boat is on the plane start to slowly trim out using the trim button. The bow will appear to rise and, as there is less water contact with the hull, the speed increases. The helm can now reduce power. The object of the exercise is to reduce the wetted surface area and, therefore, reduce friction.

Trimming in (or down) is important for:

- getting quickly up on the plane;
- pulling waterskiers;
- completing fast, tight turns;
- approaching oncoming waves.

Before you begin

Crew safety is partly a matter of being properly equipped, and partly a matter of knowing what is going on. It is of paramount importance that people should wear safety equipment, and everyone should be seated and secure whenever the boat is moving. In addition, everyone in the crew needs to be warned about any high-speed manoeuvres in advance, so that they can prepare themselves and enjoy the experience. Travelling at high speed has other risks. To avoid an obstruction in the water, for example, you may have to take action that cannot be conveyed to the crew in time for them to prepare themselves. Therefore it is also the responsibility of the crew to ensure that they remain secure and prepared for unexpected manoeuvres. Likewise, if you try to show off to your crew by flying across the waves and throwing them about, without checking that they are properly prepared, they will end up shaken, frightened and more often than not injured. Worse still, they could be overboard.

Children cannot hang on as well as adults and if young people are on board they and the adults need to be away from the front of the boat where the most movement occurs. Informing them to hang on tight is not that effective for one can only hang on tight for a short time. After bouncing over a few waves the youngsters will relax their grip and, in an instant, they will find themselves in the water.

Injuries sustained from remaining in the bow position and striking waves at speed are frequently spinal and the unfortunate crew are often left with permanent damage.

Never have young children, or adults for that matter, sitting dangling their legs over the bow. One slip and they are over the bow and through the propeller.

Avoid sitting on the side tubes of a RIB if there is no centre handhold. Rig up a cross rope as a handle. Holding the strop underneath the body with two hands will not prevent a backward somersault into the propeller on a tight turn.

An ill-prepared crew member on one boat thought that he could move position and stood up as the boat hit a wave. He was thrown onto the back of the helm's seat, breaking three of his ribs.

All crew should have handholds. This is a section of a broom handle with a piece of ski rope.

9

Once a boat is moving fast across the water, remain secure and seated. Remember that the speed across water appears to be about three times the speed over the land. This has been compared to sitting in front of a video with everything rushing towards you and flashing past. If you are not used to it, this can be a pretty alarming experience. Most inexperienced crew members feel that they are doing in excess of 40 miles per hour when in actual fact the boat has been travelling at its minimum planing speed of 15 knots (18mph).

As far as the driver is concerned, total concentration and vigilance is required at all times.

An experienced helm moulds into the boat and becomes almost part of it, similar to a motorcyclist on his bike. The helm knows when to accelerate and when to close down, when to turn and when to power straight on. He is able to judge the size and speed of the waves at a glance and detect the telltale signs of shallow water or floating hazards. But it takes hours and hours of practice to reach this level of competence. Don't fool yourself – just because the brochure says that the craft will do 50 mph, it does not mean that the driver can. Be cautious and never drive beyond your limitations. You could break something and it might be painful...

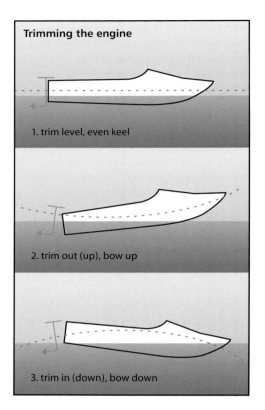

Trimming the engine

1. trim level, even keel

2. trim out (up), bow up

3. trim in (down), bow down

First time up

Think ahead about your first time up on the plane. Find space and flat water. Trim the engine down. Check all around and, if clear, start to apply a steady build up of power. The boat will start to climb the hump (the boat pushes a wall of water up under the bow – the hull has to ride over this hump), so keep building the power. The bow will rise and your vision may be impaired briefly. As the speed increases the hull will eventually come unstuck. The bow drops and the boat should now be up on the plane. However, with the engine still trimmed in, the bow will be forced down and will dig into the water. Start to trim up and free off the hull.

Once planing, somewhere in the region of 18 to 20 knots across the water, start trimming the engine up using the hydraulic trim button on the gear (trim and tilt) lever. As you start to trim up, the bow lifts and the hull frees itself from the water. The boat continues to accelerate and at this point you can bring the throttle back and maintain the planing speed.

Testing 'the set-up' of small, fast boats

Several tons of boat punching its way across a flat sea.

If the sportsboat is correctly set up and trimmed it should fly in a straight line without any tendency to pull either to port or starboard. Large engines are offset and raised to allow for the torque. Do not be too surprised, on measuring the position of the engine mounting bolts, to find the engine's position is not geometrical. The trim tab below the anti-cavitation plate should also be correctly set. If the boat is evenly balanced with the weight of crew and cargo, it should now be possible to bring it up onto the plane and, once trimmed out, to fly in a straight line without any side pressure on the helm wheel. For this test the water does need to be calm and free of traffic. If you now trim down, the boat should turn to the right as the bow digs in; if you trim back up it should go straight; and if you trim up too far it should go to the left – all without the helm turning the steering wheel. Balanced and with hands free of the helm, you should be able to throttle off and on without deviating from a straight line. Obviously you will be prepared to grab the steering wheel if you need to take control and one hand will be on the throttle control so that you can bring the power off if you need to.

If, having tested the balance and trim, you find the boat pulling to the left, even when trimmed in the up position, I suggest that the first thing to do is to readjust the position of the trim tab under the anti-cavitation plate. Loosen the holding nut and move the tab towards the bias. Opposite to the way the reader is probably thinking!

Tight turns

When using a standard sportsboat on a fairly flat sea, trim down in preparation to make the turn. Keep one hand on the wheel and the other on the throttle. Check that the area you are about to turn into is clear. Inform your crew of your intention and start the turn. Check again the area of water you are planning to turn into. As the turn tightens, the speed will drop away. Increase throttle on the turn. Keep it controlled and tight. When you exit the turn and straighten your course, trim up to free off the hull.

Ventilation

If you attempt the same exercise with the hull trimmed up, the turn will be unstable. Depending on the hull and the size of engine you may suck air in under the hull and ventilate the propeller. The propeller loses its grip (laminar flow) and spins free, the hull slips sideways and the engine peaks its rpm.

Trimmed too high

The propeller can also ventilate if you trim up too far in a straight line, causing the bow to bounce. I refer to a bouncing bow as 'porpoising.' Once the hull starts to porpoise the only way to stop it is to throttle back, trim down slightly and then once again power up.

Pooping

Another way to test a planing hull is to keep the boat travelling in a straight line, trim back down and watch the effect. As you trim down the bow will start to drop and the wave that was coming out amidships (or even further back towards the stern) will start to move forwards towards the bow.

Diabolical trim; it only planes because it has 150hp at the rear

While you are on a straight line run, throttle back a little and hold steady. The boat should slowly lose speed and come off the plane. The wave amidships moves forward and becomes a bow wave again. Now throttle back slowly until the boat stops and move the lever into neutral.

Repeat the exercise and watch the stern wave as the craft comes off the plane. As the apparent weight of the boat increases, so the stern wave increases in size. Remember this stern wave is travelling at a slower speed than the boat. Stopping slowly allows the stern wave to catch up with the boat slowly. If you throttle back from a planing mode instantly, the stern wave will surge up on you and possibly break over the stern, filling the boat with water and requiring you to work the bucket or the pump to get rid of the excess water. It is unlikely that the engine will stop as a modern engine can be dumped under water and still come up smiling. There is usually a large quantity of air under the hood and as long as the dunking last for only a second or two all should be well.

Forced forward by stern wave

The stern wave rides over the stern and will propel the boat several metres further forward. Inexperienced operators travelling too fast towards a jetty often end up ramming it. Although they probably de-throttled in good time they had not reckoned on their own stern wave picking them up and pushing them forward. As the boat is stopping, just a touch of forward throttle will move the boat away from the stern wave and prevent a swamping.

Bow ballast

Racing boats are often fitted with bow tanks. As the boat approaches the turn it scoops water up and fills a water ballast tank. This drops the bow for a fast turn. As the boat straightens out it dumps the water. A cubic metre of water weighs a metric tonne (1,000 kilos).

Trim tabs

Larger sportsboats are very susceptible to crosswinds. When on the plane they will lean into the wind and waves. The disadvantages of this are:

- It is very uncomfortable.
- The wetted surface of the hull is not of uniform shape and therefore performance is impaired.
- It is not economical.
- It is difficult to steer.
- In certain circumstances it could be dangerous.

Trim tabs can remedy all of the above.

Principles of trim tabs

Trim tabs fitted at each corner on the stern act like aerolon flaps on aircraft wings. Trim tabs should be operated by hydraulic rams. As an example, if you put the starboard trim tab down it will lift the starboard stern and push the bow down portside. Obviously if you put the port trim tab down it will force the starboard bow down. The correct use of trim tabs will set the boat up correctly across the water and stop it leaning into the wind.

Trim tabs can be used to pick the boat up onto the plane very quickly. They are also very useful where you have an imbalance of crew. Trim tab buttons and gauges can be a little confusing for the beginner. Try to have the trim buttons on the dashboard set so that if you want port bow down you push the port trim button down. In reality it will be the starboard trim tab that forces the port bow down. Cross-wire them or change over the switches.

Typical outdrive unit – freshwater flushing unit being used   *Trim tabs on the stern of the Boston Whaler*

9

Setting up the trim tabs

How do you know where the trim tabs are set? Usually the only way I can do this is by looking over the stern to find out exactly what their position is before I start out. The best way is to ask a crew member to push the switches, whilst I look over the stern until I am happy they are in the right place. You can also sort out which rocker switch works which tab. I find that there is nothing more frustrating than pushing things and then waiting for something to happen but not being quite sure what the effect is going to be.

Trim out of balance – I suggest starboard trim should be down

Trim tabs on sports cruisers

Sports cruisers built for very high speed may well require the trim tabs to be used in preparation for turning tightly to port or starboard. As an example, commencing a turn to starboard would require the helm to start turning the wheel to starboard as the starboard trim tab goes down. This flattens the hull off as it goes into a tight right turn and can prevent the hull from side slipping. The opposite action is required for a turn to port. Obviously the trim must be reset as the turn is being completed. Sportsboats lean into the turns whereas warships lean outwards.

Trim tab use in crosswinds

When you are travelling up the waves or down the waves in light conditions, the trim tabs can be set virtually level. They become really useful when you are travelling across the waves because larger sportsboats will lean into the waves and into the wind. As an example, let us assume that you are travelling at 45° into the wind direction. Example wind from the starboard shoulder of the boat at an angle of 45°. The sportsboat on the plane will have starboard side down, leaning into these waves and into the wind.

I can understand your reaction to this statement but I can assure you that I have not made a mistake. You may think that the boat would actually be leaning down to the left away from the wind and waves. However, this is not so. Trim down the starboard trim tab and the boat will flatten off, the handling will be improved, the performance of the boat will feel more secure and the trip will be much more pleasurable. Do remember when you move in another direction that you need to reset the trim tabs. The waves and troughs are moving from the right to the left.

Fixed trim tabs

I have also experienced the benefit of fixed tabs on small fast powerboats. They can be fixed and adjusted with bottle screws to a set position.

Manual lift and tilt

If your engine is a manual lift and tilt you should find a rod under the bracket holding the engine onto the back of the boat. This rod can be inserted into a selection of different holes, thereby setting the angle of the engine into the most convenient position for planing.

Because it is fixed, adjustment to trim cannot be made underway.

Small boats rely on the weight distribution of crew and cargo. Obviously, if everything was loaded into the stern it is highly unlikely that the hull will reach planing speed. You will always have to compromise.

On the plane – wave jumping and rough weather

When the waves are not too steep and not too far apart, a small high-speed planing craft can handle them at top speed, literally skimming over the top. Heavier and bigger sportsboats can handle bigger waves. Just because you have a high-speed sportsboat, it does not mean that you can travel flat out in every direction you wish to go. In the rough you may be reduced to a maximum speed of 5 knots.

Downwind and upwind

If the tide is travelling with the wind you will have a fairly easy ride, but if the tide is moving against the wind the waves will be blowing in steep, sharp peaks and the ride will be hard and lumpy.

You may have to slow down. Travelling into the wind and therefore into the waves, trim the engine down to lift the stern and force the bow through the waves. Do not trim in the up position thinking that you can take a softer option. It is necessary for the bow – the sharp bit – to pierce the wave to give a comfortable ride.

When travelling down the waves do exactly the opposite. If you are riding on the back of the wave in the direction the wave is going with the wind in the same direction as travel, trim up. It keeps the bow up. Then sit on the back of the wave if you can, until you are happy you can go over the top into the trough in front and then up the back of the next wave. Throttle control is important. Generally speaking, the speed going down the waves is going to be far greater than the speeds going against the waves.

Negotiating big waves requires a different technique. Instead of skimming across the crest the boat will ride up and over each wave individually. Get it wrong and the boat may flip over or plunge through the wave instead of over it. Big waves require clever throttle control. A comfortable ride now depends on the type of boat you are using. In big waves a small sportsboat could easily be sunk; the bow will dig into the wave in front, the wave will come over the top of the bow, hit the windshield and land in your lap. All this water coming into the boat has to be quickly removed before the next wave comes over.

9

If you are doing the same exercise in a rigid inflatable boat (RIB), you will find that a passage can be just as wet but that all the water taken over the bow and into the boat is easily removed by the self-balers at the transom. RIBs offer massive amounts of buoyancy and lift and, in my view, will always handle heavy conditions better than a sportsboat.

First of Honda's formula 4-strokes on test in Poole Harbour, with 130hp

Rough weather without trim

If you are using a RIB and are heading into the waves without the ability to alter the trim, move your crew forward. When travelling down the waves, move the crew towards the stern. The movement of the crew will effectively operate in a similar way to the trim tabs or engine trim. Do try to avoid going ahead into a wave that is breaking. The breaking crest is the release of energy and if this wave is not met exactly on the bow the boat can be swept sideways and rolled over. Better still go for the area of the wave that does not have a breaking crest. Heavy weather can be frightening so avoid it if at all possible.

Reducing the slam

Try lengthening the distance between the peaks of the waves by crossing them slightly off centre. The hull slides along the top of the wave and softens the drop. Several waves can be taken to the right followed by a similar number to the left. In this way your ship's heading can be maintained

Flying a hull

Travelling very fast across the water is literally flying a hull. The real exhilaration is when there is very little hull in the water. Sometimes it is just the propeller that bites into the water and at other times, if the conditions are right, the whole hull will lift out of the water completely and fly. Being airborne is not a problem, but landing back on the water can be. Not all boats can handle this type of treatment – nor can the crew, for that matter.

For example, a 24ft (7.5m) Tornado, lightly loaded and pushed along by a Yamaha 200, will literally bound off the back of a wave and fly. It will stay tilted in the air at the angle of lift-off until it re-enters the water. The boat will instantly straighten itself, ready for the next lift-off. Sheer exhilaration and a great feeling of safety.

Spray rails

Underneath a performance hull there are spray rails, which are ridges for directional stability. At speed some hulls rock back and forth on their chines or spray rails. In some cases the rocking movements may become quite violent and dangerous. Once the hull starts rocking from side to side, trim down and slow down.

Once balance has been regained, power up. But if the rocking continues you may need to investigate the engine set-up and weight distribution. You may also need to consider fixed trim tabs, and you may have to put a smaller engine on the transom.

Throttle control
The object at high speed is to keep the propeller in contact with the water. The rpm of the propeller is governed by the amount of water resistance passing across the blades. Ventilation and cavitation is the breakdown of this laminar flow, and the propeller slips, a little like car tyres on ice.

When the propeller slips, for whatever reason, it is unlikely to recover its thrust until the laminar flow can be re-established. Therefore throttle back off the power and only reapply power once the propeller has gripped. The same applies when you are airborne with the propeller out of the water. Throttle back before the stern re-enters the water. It can save the gearbox from destruction.

9

10 Man Overboard (MOB)

This is a Honda race boat; when hammering a wave in a tight turn, crew have been known to leave the boat!

This is a serious situation that should never arise. You should try to make sure that it never happens by avoiding some, if not all, of the following situations:

- Crew not secure before moving away.
- Accelerating too fast.
- Rough conditions.
- Travelling too fast for the conditions.
- Mechanical failure – usually steering controls – owing to poor maintenance.
- Messing about in boats – they are not toys!
- Striking a hazard.
- Incorrect approach to mooring, jetty or pontoon.
- Collision.
- Sunbathing or sitting on the foredeck or bow.
- Changing over seating arrangements whilst under way.
- Catching a rope round a propeller; the sudden de-acceleration may put a person over the side – usually the bow.
- Making exceptionally steep turns, thereby putting a person over the side.
- Unexpected impact with wave on a turn.
- Leaning over being seasick; crew should hold the person's lifejacket to prevent MOB.

- Crew very cold (hypothermia) leading to disorientation.
- Alcohol- or drug-related reasons.

Even if you take every precaution, you may still make a miscalculation one day and find yourself or a crew member toppling over the side. Also it is not an uncommon occurrence for a sailor to slip off the pontoon at night, on returning from the local public house or club bar. It is only in the last few years that marinas have placed ladders at the ends of their pontoons so people can climb out of the water.

10

You – the man overboard

If you feel yourself slipping off the side of the boat do not hang on; you may be dragged under the boat towards the propeller. Let go and throw yourself clear.

- Shout as you fall overboard. Crew may well be looking forwards and it is possible to slip over the side unnoticed. Close your mouth when you hit the water.
- Inflate your lifejacket (not applicable if you are wearing a buoyancy jacket) if needed. You show up better if the jacket is inflated, especially if the water is choppy, and you also sit higher in the water.
- Remain calm; you will be disorientated when you rise to the surface. If there are waves combined with swell, do not be surprised if you are unable to see the boat you have just fallen from.
- Remain completely still and allow the lifejacket to bring you to the surface with your head above water (stabilise your position in the water). Remaining still will also enable you to adjust to the water temperature better than if you are floundering around.
- Check yourself over; hitting the water at speed resembles an impact with a brick wall.
- Indicate that all is well, to the boat if you can.

Whatever happens, remain calm. Do not swim around or make for the shore. Swimming around only puts you out of position for pickup. Anyway, where are you going to swim to? Remain in place and await the return of the boat. You will drift with the current and when the boat comes alongside you and stops, it too will drift with the current.

Any water temperature below 68°F (20°C) is considered to be cold. To maintain warmth, remain still and bring your knees up slightly towards the surface. Hold the inner sides of your arms against the sides of your chest, keeping your hands down in your groin area, and keep your thighs pressed together. Alternatively, just lie back with your hands on the top part of your jacket and your elbows tucked into your side. This position helps to minimise the loss of vital body heat and permits a person to survive approximately one-third longer than if he or she was treading water. Do not go into a rolled ball position with legs up and tucked in as it restricts the blood flow and, more importantly, the wave movement can roll you over.

If you are not wearing a lifejacket or buoyancy aid, you will have to tread water, moving your arms and legs just enough to keep your head above water. Because of this limb movement you will lose body heat and energy much faster than if you keep still. You may not be able to make coordinated leg and arm movements for more than 10 minutes in water with a temperature of less than 50°F (10°C).

Watch for the approach of the boat.

Stabilise your position and wait.

Collecting the MOB

As soon as the cry goes out 'man overboard', check astern and locate the position of the MOB. If possible, detail one member of the party to point continually at the MOB. Do not take your eyes off the MOB, not even for a second. In heavy seas you may only see the MOB once every 10 seconds. If you are now the only person left on board you will have to keep the MOB in sight yourself. Slow down and, as you maintain control of the craft, turn the same side as the person who has fallen overboard (see note). Try not to spin the craft around as distance can be a help in positioning for collection of the MOB.

Thumbs up or the "OK" fingers helps the crew on board.

Check wind direction by noting the direction of the waves. Manoeuvre the craft into a wide circle in preparation for approaching the MOB. Continue to maintain visual contact with the MOB. There are several alternative methods of coming alongside a person in the water. Three of them are covered below.

Drift onto MOB

The 'drift on' method is ideal for boats above 18–20ft (5–6m) in length and where the wind strength does not exceed Force 4.

As soon as the cry 'man overboard' goes out, gain control of the boat, slow down and establish wind direction. If the waves have sharp edges they are moving towards you. If the waves have soft edges they are going away from you.

Bring the boat around so that the boat is parallel to the waves and between the wind and the

Don't ever take your eye off the MOB or fail to point at it's last known position.

person in the water. The wind effect on the boat is far greater than the wind effect on the person. Therefore the boat will drift down onto the person. Remember that different hull shapes sit at different angles to the wind. You will need to adjust your angle of approach accordingly.

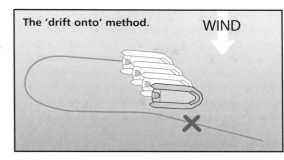

The 'drift onto' method.   WIND

10

Recovery can then be made. (See Recovery, page 96).

Heavy weather

It is quite possible that the conditions are too bad to place a boat broadside to the wind in case it capsizes. The drift-on method means that you are working with the MOB to leeward and putting your weight over the leeward side to collect the MOB.

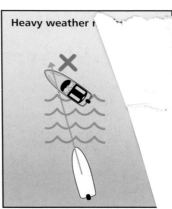

Heavy weather

As soon as the cry 'man overboard' is heard, place the boat under control and ensure that a crew member is pointing at the MOB.

Immediately consider notifying the Coastguard of your predicament.

Assess the wind and wave direction, turn the same side as the person who has fallen overboard and bring the boat around into a sweeping circle, so that it is downwind of the person in the water.

Some 160ft (50m) back from the person in the water reduce the speed to tick over, or a speed manageable for the conditions, and slowly approach into the waves, taking them on the bow but with a slight bias to port. The MOB will be drifting in the waves towards you. Aim to come alongside on the starboard side (if you are helming from the starboard side position).

Go into neutral and allow the weight of the boat to carry you the last few metres. If you are picking up on starboard, spin the top of the wheel to port. This kicks the back of the boat slightly towards the MOB and puts the wind and wave on the starboard bow. As soon as contact is made, SWITCH OFF THE ENGINE. As the MOB makes contact and holds onto the side of the boat, their legs will swing under the hull and down towards the propeller. If the engine is still switched on and in gear, the consequences could be very nasty.

Lean over the starboard side and grab the hand or lifejacket of the MOB.

Obviously, the boat will continue to turn broadside into the waves. However, all the weight this time is on the windward side, including the MOB, and there is less chance of capsize.

Very heavy weather
In very heavy weather MOB pickup is not only dangerous to the MOB but also to the crew of the sportsboat. Maintain watch on the person in the water. With the boat under control keep the bows working into the waves. Notify the Coastguard of your position and circumstances and inform them that you will carry out a recovery (PAN PAN).

Radio first and then choose the moment to turn correctly in the waves. Circle and stand into the waves (bow into wind) as the MOB is brought down to you. If you are in a rigid inflatable boat in excess of 22–23ft (6–7m) in length, collect the person on the shoulder of the boat and bring them aboard.

IMPORTANT NOTE – THIS IS NOT FOR PRACTICE

The coxswain may have to maintain control by using forward gear. The risk involved is obvious. Being broadside to a rough sea could be dangerous and if a switched-off engine fails to start it could have serious consequences for all concerned. The boat has to be long enough for the shoulder pickup to be a good distance from the propeller/s. The manning level must be trained coxswain plus at least two trained crew.

As soon as collection has been made notify Coastguard. (When you inform the Coastguard initially of your situation they open a log and wait for you to close that log. If, for any reason, you are turned upside down in the course of recovery and are unable to send a message, the Coastguard are in a position to render assistance.)

A conventional sportsboat will probably be hard sided with a bathing platform at the stern. In rough conditions, you may have to stand off the MOB because the bow and stern are pitching so high that – if you were to put the boat into the wrong position – it would be possible to crash down onto the MOB. You may be able to recover the MOB successfully by streaming floating lines astern of the powerboat. (Watch the props!) The powerboat maintains way into the waves and manoeuvres slightly as the MOB drifts past, hoping that the MOB will catch one of the lines and, with help, draw themself towards the stern of the boat. At the last moment, engines neutral and then switched off!

TOP TIPS

1   If you are carrying out any exercises of this nature in a training group, please inform either the harbour authority or the Coastguard of your intentions. They will want to know time, place, number of boats and people, who is in charge and their qualifications. They will require notification that the exercises have been completed.

2   If you just want to practise the MOB manoeuvre I suggest you find a suitable area of water and lob over the side a half-filled plastic bottle. Don't take your eyes off it and don't lose it because plastic bottles are not biodegradable.

3   If you are working from a high-sided boat, tie a loop of rope around the handle of the bottle and use a boathook to collect it.

4   Hard-hulled sports boats and cruisers have the shiny sides and no handholds. Quickly attach fenders along the side next to the casualty for grabbing.

10

People may say that switching off the engine/s in rough conditions is a questionable action, as being sideways or beam onto large waves can turn a craft over. In my opinion, the experienced helm must assess the risk at the time, taking into consideration all eventualities, and cannot be guided by the written word. Whatever action is taken may be open to criticism if things go wrong!

Sector search

It may well be that you are called to an area where a MOB has been lost from a boat and asked to assist in recovery. It could be that a search is being carried out because sighting of the MOB has been lost. There are two search patterns that can be adopted – the box sectional search and the sector search. I will deal with the sector search.

Radio through the circumstances and explain your intentions. Move into the area where the person has been lost. Using available navigational aids try to locate your boat very close to the original MOB position. If you are using a GPS MOB button, it will only be of use for the very first part of a sector search. On a heading north 000/360° drop a marker (dan buoy) into the water. Maintain a heading north whilst keeping an eye on the dan buoy. As you move away keep a count in seconds until the dan buoy or floating mark can be only seen for 50% of the time because it is obscured by distance or waves. Don't change the throttle setting at any time.

Whatever the count in seconds round it up to an easy number and then double this number. In this example, I am using a dipping count of 50. Double this number and add it to the 50, making a total count time of 150. Continue to travel north for the total number of seconds counted, i.e. 150.

At the count of 150, turn immediately to starboard to a new heading of 120° magnetic. Continue on this new heading for the total count of 150.

At the count of 150 turn sharply 120° to starboard, giving yourself a new heading of 240°, and continue for the count of 150. This heading will take you close to the original mark that you dropped. You should see the floating dan buoy at around the count of 75. Once it is spotted, alter course if necessary to pass close by. At the mark continue on the original heading of 240° for another count of 150.

At the completion of the count turn smartly through 120° to starboard. This brings you on a new heading of 000° (360° north), which was the heading you first started on.

At the count of 150 turn 120° to starboard and keep travelling on this new heading of 120° magnetic for a count of 150. Again it will take you back past or close to the original marker dropped. At the mark, or in proximity to the mark, continue the count of 150 on this bearing of 120° magnetic.

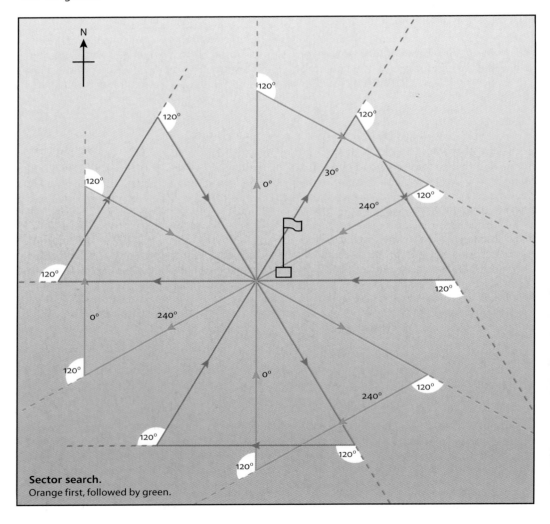

Sector search.
Orange first, followed by green.

At the completion of the count of 150, turn smartly to starboard on a new heading 240° magnetic. At the count of 150, turn smartly through 120° to starboard. This gives you a new heading of 360° and should line you up on your original starter heading pointing north. This should bring you back close to the mark. You have now completed three sets of triangles using the marker as your pivot point.

Once the first circuit has been completed and you are back to your position at the dan buoy, recommence the triangles but this time offset by 30°. In other words your heading from the marker now becomes 030°magnetic for a count of 150, and when you put the first turn of 120° to starboard your new heading will become 150°. Your next heading will then become 270° and so on. Another set of triangles will now be imposed over the first set. The result should complete coverage of the area in which the MOB has taken place.

When carrying out this exercise you need to note the following points:

- The MOB button on a GPS will bring you to the original point, but wind and water will have moved the MOB since then. It is important, therefore, only to use the GPS position for the first occasion when you drop the marker buoy.

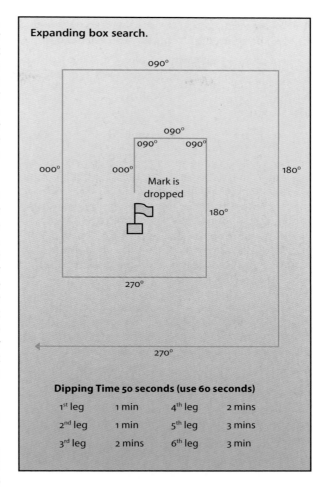

Expanding box search.

Dipping Time 50 seconds (use 60 seconds)			
1st leg	1 min	4th leg	2 mins
2nd leg	1 min	5th leg	3 mins
3rd leg	2 mins	6th leg	3 min

- The wind will move the boat off course in a different way to the wind effect on the MOB.

- It is very likely that on completion of the first triangle you may not have found the marker. Maintain discipline and run the second and third sets of triangles. The wind will move you one way and then the other depending on what leg of the triangle you are running. In practice, I have often only discovered the marker after completing the last leg of the final triangle.

- Only use the steering compass. Do not line up the bow on adjacent land or fixed objects. Land and fixed objects do not drift with the wind and current and therefore your position will be a long way out on completion.

- Tidy tight turns and accurate compass work and helming are essential.
- It is important to maintain an accurate count.
- Scribble the triangles on a piece of paper and tick them off. This could be pre-arranged and kept on board. The final search pattern may well be several miles away from the original position of the MOB, so it is essential to ensure that you are not being drifted onto or into areas of danger.

Recovery

Recovery into a rubber inflatable boat should be easy. Lift and roll the MOB over the side and inboard. If the MOB is heavy and difficult to lift, inflate their lifejacket (if worn) and, having first warned them of your intentions, turn them so their back is to the boat. Place your hand on their head, force them under the water and release them. The MOB will pop out of the water like a rubber ball, and you can catch them and lift them over the side and into the boat. It sounds very easy until you actually try it. A lot depends on the height of the tube above the water. It is very difficult to lift the person high enough for their backside to sit on the tube. If the person is recovered backwards and dragged over the boat at least their head is back and the airway is open.

If the MOB is injured, it may be possible to let some of the air out of one of the side tubes in the inflatable. This makes it easier to roll the injured person inboard. Your tool kit should include a pump so that you can replace the air in the tube after the recovery. However, most inflatables should remain operational with one or more compartments deflated.

It is a good idea to keep ropes, snap-shackled to the edge of the boat, to use as grab handles. One of these can be dropped as a loop under the water for the MOB to stand in. Again sounds easy until you try it. It reminds me of attempting to climb a rope ladder up a tree; wherever you put your foot, the ladder shoots away from you. With inflatables you can recover via the stern of the craft (see below).

Roll casualty on board, head to stern.   Bounce the casualty to gain the lift for back entry to boat.

Solid hull

Recovery over the side of a small powerboat can be a problem. The hard sides also make it painful. Having approached the MOB and made contact, you can always use a rope or fender to prevent the MOB from sliding along the smooth length of the hull.

The ladder at the stern of the powerboat would appear to be the ideal recovery aid, but in practice the it does not always go deep enough into the water. The MOB will have to kneel on the bottom rung and kneeling on a metal rod is painful. If you fit some padding to the bottom rung, it will make the ladder more comfortable for bathers, too.

10

I recommend that the MOB should be taken to the stern of the boat using the fender and then use the bathing platform or climbing ladder. If you have neither, encourage the MOB to use the anti-cavitation plate above the propeller as a step. Care must be taken because if the MOB slips off the anti-cavitation plate their foot will go directly onto the sharp edges of the propeller. You may read in other publications that this method is not to be attempted. However, if it results in the safe recovery of a MOB in a real situation then it must be useful. It is obvious that the engine must be switched off.

With the power unit switched off the boat will lie across the waves or with bow downwind. The stern can therefore be a reasonably safe place to board. With the boat broadside the bow and stern should not be crashing up and down. Attempting to recover somebody amidships over a traditional sportsboat is exceedingly difficult. It may be necessary to put a small tender into the water first or then try to place the MOB on a smaller floatation device before trying to get them into the boat.

Straight forward lift over the side of the boat.

Always consider placing a cold casualty in a survival bag or equivalent. Don't forget the hat!

Problems

Injured MOB

The various methods of recovery discussed above are only practical if the MOB is able to assist. What if they are injured or unconscious? This is not such an acute problem with an inflatable boat, since you can recover them by letting air out of one of the side tanks. A recovery into a solid hull boat is much more difficult.

First secure the MOB to the side of the craft to stop them floating away. Then, if the MOB is not wearing a lifejacket or personal floatation device (PFD) they must be fitted with one. This could mean a second person has to enter the water. Do be cautious when making this decision. Carefully assess the risk giving consideration to the following:

- Is the second person correctly dressed?

- Are they attached to a lifeline?

- Will it be possible for the second person to return aboard without creating undue problems?

- Can the person entering the water perform artificial resuscitation if need be?

- Will entering the water put the second person's life at risk or put the remaining crew and boat at risk?

All flares are used down wind, including rockets. In this demonstration, it is held down to prevent attracting detection (inland).

It is a difficult decision to make, and you need to make it fast. Personally, I would always try to avoid a second person entering the water.

You need assistance

Let us set a scene.

The MOB is alongside, secure and floating with the aid of a lifejacket. The MOB is breathing, but you have failed to get them into the boat. If you try to tow them ashore they could well slip into the propeller, the bow wave could drown them or, at the very least, the movement through the water would quickly drain away their body heat and they would die from hypothermia. You need help, and speed is of the essence. You must therefore attract the attention of other craft in the vicinity by radio or by one of the following distress signals:

- Sound – whistle, foghorn, shouting.

- Visual – torchlight for Morse code; slowly raising and lowering your arms while facing other boats.

- Flares – orange smoke, which is used in daylight and can be seen in reasonable visibility 3–4 miles (4–6km) away; a red hand flare, which can be seen for approximately the same distance at night; a rocket, which rises to approximately 1,000m (3,000ft) before releasing a flare on a parachute, which falls to earth burning for approximately 40 seconds. Visibility in good conditions is 25 miles (40km) plus. Another useful flare is the anti-collision flare, which is white and designed to be used where a craft needs to make its position clear to other users. White flares should be carried on very small boats, dinghies and canoes where they might be run down in open water.

10

Radio – for messages to other vessels and the Coastguard. (VHF message PAN PAN Man Overboard). Anyone coming to your assistance will need to know the name and colour of your vessel and your approximate position. Remember that if you give latitude and longitude as your position, not everyone will be able to disseminate this information. It may well be better to give an approximate position off a headland or close to a charted object. As an example, 'three miles south of such and such lighthouse' will give

The best means of communication.

the rescue services a good idea as to the position of your boat. If you are taking a bearing off a lighthouse or headland you will need to add or subtract 180° to this bearing to give the rescuers an idea of your location. In other words, give the back bearing (reciprocal bearing). If the lighthouse has a bearing from your position of say, 245° your position from the lighthouse would be 245 minus 180, i.e. 065°

Satellite navigation will obviously give you a very accurate latitude and longitude position.

Mobile phone – mobile phones have been very successful in aiding recovery out on the water. I would suggest that if this is your only means of communication you program the emergency telephone numbers into the machine for Coastguard, harbour master etc, plus 999, so that you can activate them quickly. Mobile phones are susceptible to water and dampness and should be placed in a sealed plastic bag similar to the type used for hand-held radios. The downside to using mobile phones is that no other person can hear the conversation and the location of the phone cannot be identified from RDF (Radio Direction Finding). It is far better to use a marine VHF.

Having made contact
Let us assume you make contact and professional assistance is to hand. The rescue boat will come alongside. Await instructions.

If it is not a professional rescue team you will have to coordinate rescue and work together. Your next move depends on the type of vessel that has come to your aid. If it is a small powerboat you will simply benefit from the extra physical strength of its crew. A larger powerboat may have davits at the stern with a small boat hanging from them. Use this to scoop the MOB from the water.

If a sailing yacht offers assistance, this is fortuitous since yachts are fully equipped with excellent means to lift people out of the water, such as the mainsheet on the block and tackle at the end of the boom and make sails secure. Release the mainsheet from the deck. Tie the rope to the MOB's lifejacket, or around the MOB using a bowline. You can use a halyard intended for lifting a sail in much the same way, employing a winch to lift the MOB out of the water and onto the yacht. Alternatively, you may be able to drop a sail into the water, still attached to the top of the mast by the halyard, slide the MOB into the sail and winch them up, taking care that they are not injured by the stanchions and lifelines as they are rolled inboard onto the yacht. Many yachts have recovery aids for lifting people out of the water.

In extremis

If you have any concern regarding your ability to collect the MOB you must immediately inform the Coastguard and request assistance. If there is no help nearby and you cannot get your casualty aboard, then you will quickly have to resort to professional rescue services. The best and most effective way of summoning such help is by radio. You should attend a course to gain a certificate of competence in handling VHF radios. A recognised course in First Aid is also highly recommended.

Night rescue

More and more sportsboats are being used at night. It is important, therefore, that one or two extra considerations are taken prior to setting out. Refer to the equipment list on pages 29-30 for a list of essential items. All lifejackets must have lights or strobes fitted to them to be used in an emergency. All lifejackets must also have reflective tape attached to them and conform to the latest EC regulations. The reflective tape is picked up in the torchlight or spotlight. With light-reflective tape and a strobe light on the lifejacket and by using a night scope, an MOB recovery should be as possible and successful at night as it is in the daytime.

Williamson turn

If you are running a large boat at displacement speed the following exercise may be of use to you.

As soon as the shout 'man overboard' is heard put the helm over to the same side as the MOB. Keep the helm over and the engine speed constant for an alteration of compass course of roughly 60° from the ship's original heading. As the compass swings onto this new heading, put the helm over to the opposite lock and hold it there for a course

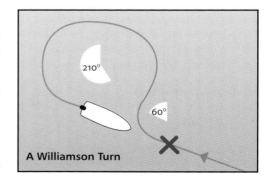

A Williamson Turn

change of approximately 210°. When you reach this course, cut the power and allow the boat to drift down to the MOB. They should, by now, be directly ahead. When close, send out a swimmer attached by a lifeline to collect the MOB or lower a boat, which is slower but much safer.

This method has been recognised by users of larger craft and fishing boats for some considerable time.

If you are attempting this as a practice exercise in a small sportsboat you will need only half helm to starboard and then half helm to port at displacement speed. Because the sportsboat is light in weight it will not complete the full manoeuvre. It will come to rest pointing at the MOB, but several metres away.

10

Ropes used in recovery

As an aid to bringing a MOB closer to a stationary boat, do consider throwing a rope. All ropes should be coiled correctly and when thrown should go out the full length of the line. The heaving line should float in the water to give the MOB the best chance of recovery.

If you position the boat upwind of the casualty the rope will always travel more easily than if the rope is thrown against the wind. The waves and wind help to carry the end of the rope down towards the person.

MOB recovery is really the ultimate test of a good powerboat handler. I use it for the final practical assessment of a candidate. If all of the above in its various forms is practised and thought through it then becomes an integral part of powerboating. All the handling characteristics at high speed and low speed are used. Observation of the wind and current awareness is important. Assessment of the surroundings and use of drift is essential. The

Don't let go and don't follow into the water!

importance of the position of the propeller is brought home. If the exercises are practised on a regular basis your boat handling ability will be enhanced, which will benefit you and your family or team. Never practise with real people – the crew should remain inside the boat and not outside.

11 Charts and buoyage

Part of the fun of boating is planning the trip

Like most powerboat users you will probably spend a lot of time in home waters that you know fairly well, but eventually you may want to venture further afield. You will need to know where you can go and where you can't, and you will also need some means of judging your position out there on the open water. For this you must know something about charts, buoys and pilotage.

Stand amongst a group of people in a marina and at the very first mention of the word 'navigation' someone will pull a hand-held GPS out of his pocket. GPS is no longer the secondary means of navigation; in some cases it is the only means of navigation. However, there are many people out on the water who just trust in their GPS without having any basic knowledge of navigation. GPS teaches one very little about navigation. It must be used with care and as a supportive instrument to traditional and tested methods.

The grid-line system

The Earth is divided by grid lines. One set of grid lines runs parallel to the Equator and are known as lines of latitude. Another set of grid lines runs vertically around the world. These grid lines start at the South Pole and end at the North Pole and are known as lines of longitude.

The lines of longitude are like the segments of a chocolate orange. All the lines meet at the poles, which means that the lines are not parallel and the distance between them varies. The lines of latitude, on the other hand, are like a hard-boiled egg that has been cut through with an egg slicer – each horizontal slice is the same thickness apart.

11

Datums

We must have a starting point, or datum, to work from. The line at the Equator is nought. Draw a circle on a piece of paper and mark a centre point on the line of the Equator with a pencil. Place a protractor on the pencil mark along the Equator line and, using the outside edge of the protractor as the curve of the Earth, mark off 10°, 20°, 30° and so on, travelling north from the Equator until you reach 90°, which is the North Pole.

Do likewise working south. You should now have half of the Earth's globe marked off in 10° sections – 180° from the North Pole to the South Pole. Place a parallel rule on the line of the Equator and draw horizontal lines at 10°, 20°, 30° and so on, moving up to the North Pole and then do exactly the same travelling south 10°, 20°, 30°, 40° and so on. You have now drawn in the lines of latitude upon a circle.

However, the Earth is not round; it is flattened off at the poles and bulges out at the Equator. It therefore follows that the distance between the Equator 'zero' and 10° is going to be different from the distance between, say 70° and 80°. But because the imaginary centre of the Earth is used as the centre point of reference for marking the degrees towards the north and south of the Equator, the distance on the Earth's surface can be accurately measured.

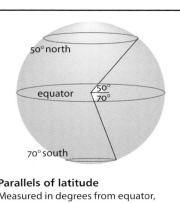

Parallels of latitude
Measured in degrees from equator,
eg 50° N or 70° S.
Up to 90°. 1 degree = 60 minutes (1° = 60')
Minutes are than divided into
tenths or hundredths,
eg 50°37'.62 N.

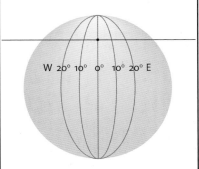

Meridians of longitude
0° goes through Greenwich, E and W measured from there (up to 180°). eg 100 25'.37 E

Latitude

I am now going to explain the system in reverse. Every 10° of (parallel) latitude represents 600 nautical miles. It therefore follows that each degree on the Earth's surface represents 60 miles. We break each degree down into 60 minutes, with each minute representing 1 nautical mile. Each minute is split into a further 60 parts for accuracy and each one of these individual parts is referred to as a second. There are therefore 60 seconds in a minute and 60 minutes in a degree.

Because it is a true measurement extending from the centre of the Earth to the edge of the Earth (when viewed travelling vertically) and because the Earth is not round, a minute of latitude at the Equator is around 6046' in length. Towards the poles a minute of latitude is in the region of 6108'. The international length of a nautical mile is averaged at 6076'. But on the south coast of England, for example, a reference to 1 nautical mile is 6080' in length.

The longitude scale is of no useful value when it comes to measuring distances. Using longitude the distance at the Equator is approximately 6076' in length, whereas at the two poles it is zero. You can now see the importance of measuring distance from the side of the chart, vertically.

Exercise
The very first thing I do when I use a powerboat in any part of the world is to obtain the largest scale chart of the area I can find and look at the latitude scale. I locate the largest figure. This will be the degrees and I then have some idea of my position on the face of the Earth.

Open up a chart of your area and look at the side of the chart. Locate the largest figure on the side of your chart. A large-scale chart will give you a greater distance between each degree and you will be able to measure the degrees, minutes and seconds more accurately.

Find your position and mark it with a small cross in pencil. Place one point of a pair of dividers onto the nearest parallel line of latitude below the small cross (in the northern hemisphere). Open the divider until you can place the other point on the marked cross. Keep the dividers vertical to

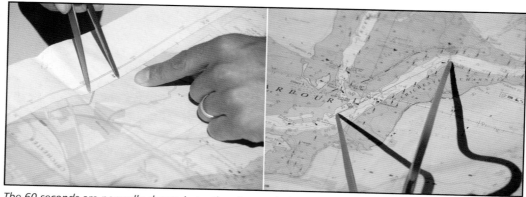

The 60 seconds are normally shown in tenths of a nautical mile (each 1/10 equals 6 seconds of latitude).

the chart. Now slide the divider from this point across to the right- or left-hand side of the chart, whichever is easiest for you.

Be careful as you move across to keep the point of the divider close to the line that you started from. You have now taken your marked cross to the side of the chart and are in a position to be able read off the accurate position of latitude. The first figure to read off is the largest figure you originally found on the side of your chart. In the example I am using, it is 50°. If you look at the side of the chart you will find some smaller figures. These refer to the minutes. My chart starts at 44' minutes and as I move north I read 45', 46', 47' and so on to 48'. In this example, we now have 50°48' (north of the Equator).

For accuracy I now need to find the position of my marked spot in relation to seconds. There are 60 seconds in a minute but most large-scale charts split the minutes into tenths. Each tenth represents 6 seconds. Using the tenths you will see that we are now fractionally over 3 1/2 tenths north of 48 minutes. Therefore it reads 50° 48'.36 north of the Equator. If we were to draw a line from here it would go all the way around the Earth, parallel to the Equator back to exactly the same spot.

Longitude

We now need to locate the vertical position to make our position accurate. The datum line for this grid reference is GMT (Greenwich Mean Time). Again GMT is referred to as zero, line 0 or 000 line. It has three noughts because one can move 180° east or 180° west and the GPS is a computer that uses three digits. Longitude is a totally different system to the parallels of latitude.

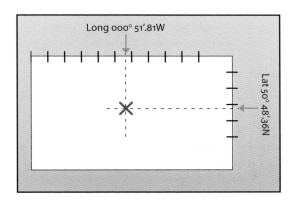

Looking down on the North Pole for example, the pole becomes the centre of a circle, and the circle is split into 360°. GMT is at 0 and from GMT moving westward the Earth is split accurately into – and I will use 10° segments – 10°, 20°, 30°, 40° and so on until we reach 180° west. The same is true travelling east from Greenwich, i.e. 10°, 20°, 30° through to 180°. The segments meet at the Date Line. Remember that all these lines of longitude join at the North Pole and South Pole. The only time they could be used as an accurate scale for measuring distance is when one is fairly close to the Equator. Here they are approximately the same distance apart as the lines of latitude.

11

Exercise

Return to the chart and look at the grid system along the top or bottom. Look for the largest figure. On the chart I am using it is 1° west from Greenwich. If you look at the minutes you will see that they are building from the right-hand side of the chart towards the left side of the chart. We are moving toward the west and again they are building 10°, 20, 30, 40°, 50° and so on up to 180°. If you were working in the eastern section of the Earth then they would be building towards the east, i.e. 10°, 20°, 30°, 40° and so on until 180° from left to right.

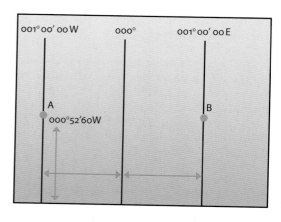

Using the dividers, put one point on the nearest line of longitude and then, keeping parallel, spread the dividers until the other point arrives at the mark on the chart. Having made sure that you have taken the accurate position, slide the dividers either to the top or bottom scale of the chart, keeping the longitude line as the reference point. Now measure off as you did on the latitude scale. In the example I have used, my position has not yet reached 1° west from Greenwich and so it is 000° 52'.60 W from Greenwich (it must be accurate). We now have the latitude scale which is 50° 48'.36 N and underneath it we have written 000° 52'.60 W. This is a unique reference point on the face of the Earth and if it is placed into a GPS receiver it could become a waypoint (WP⊞). However, before you load this Lat./Long WP into the satellite navigator refer to the GPS manual.

GPS set-up mode

Go into set-up mode and check that the degrees and seconds are actually working in tenths of a minute and not in the seconds mode. In other words, if you are using six-tenths you would put it in as .60 but if you are using seconds it would be .36 seconds (each tenth represents 6 seconds).

Whilst in set-up mode, check that you are working in nautical miles and not land miles or kilometres. The successful operation of a GPS requires accuracy with the latitude and longitude.

Only by continual practice will you become proficient, and by becoming proficient you will become safe. Check, check and double check and never take somebody else's WP as being correct. A 50° south instead of a 50° north is a long way out. In fact this error is so large that the GPS will often refuse to accept it as a reference position.

A few common errors

This list of a few of the most common errors will give you some idea of what to avoid:

- Confusing the degrees and minutes.
- When using the latitude scale of degrees as the datum point, it is important to look at the minutes

and ensure that they are greater than 0 and less than 59.99. It is only at 59.99 + minutes that the degree figure changes up 1°.

- Working down the page in the northern hemisphere and up the page in the southern hemisphere. Always increase numerically in the correct direction.

- With latitude the errors are normally east or west. For instance, GMT passes very close to Newhaven on the south coast of England and so it is easy to move from the eastern side of Greenwich to the western side of Greenwich. The difference between 1° west and 1° east is considerable.

- Recording the tenths and minutes in the wrong direction. Again always ensure that the figures are building and increasing in the direction you are moving your dividers.

Navigating with GPS

Suppose you want to navigate to a buoy, which we'll call A. Enter the latitude and longitude of A in the GPS as a waypoint. If you press "Goto A" the GPS has its current lat and long from the satellites, 'draws' an imaginary line from there to A, and gives you a bearing (in degrees True) and distance from where you are to A. In theory you just motor down that line – the GPS will even tell you the ETA at A too. But beware –

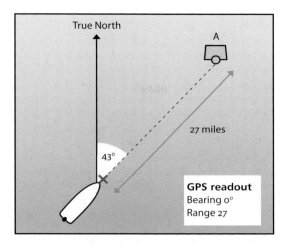

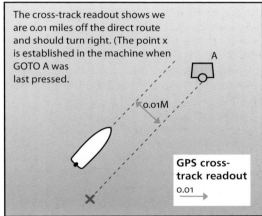

- The bearing is in degrees True, unless you set the machine otherwise
- It gives you the straight line route – even if this is over rocks, shallows – or land!
- Do not make a lighthouse, or anything solid, the waypoint – you might just hit it!

The cross track is most useful. This is your distance off the direct route. Steer to minimise the cross track and you will automatically compensate for wind, tide etc.

Charts

It is very difficult to handle a chart in a small boat. Very few sportsboats have any space where you can lay out a chart without it blowing away or getting soaked. Yet it is always wise to keep an up-to-date chart of the area somewhere on the boat. Since conventional paper charts fall to pieces when wet, it is a good idea to buy the new all-weather waterproof charts. You can keep the chart fixed to a clipboard or, better still, covered in transparent plastic sheeting. You could keep several sheets like this in book form. One of the best methods I have found is to heatseal the charts in plastic; there are laminators that deal with large sheets.

Charts come in all scales. The really small-scale ones are intended for ocean passages; these are of no use in small powerboats. You need large-scale charts of estuaries, harbours and coasts that show the mudbanks, sandbanks, buoys, channels, jetties, marinas and a host of other features in detail.

Depth of water

One of the main functions of a chart is to indicate the depth of water. It does this by a system of contour lines similar to those used on land maps to indicate heights above sea level. On a chart the depths are measured from a zero point known as Chart Datum (CD). It is also known as Lowest Astronomical Tide (LAT).

The CD on the chart has been corrected for the area and adjusted to zero. (Different charts in different areas have different datums.) Depths are measured in metres or tenths of a metre. (Fathoms –6'– will only be found on old charts). The units used are indicated at the top and bottom of the chart.

Soundings and drying areas

There are two types of figure dealing with depth: a sounding or depth below Chart Datum and drying height, which is the height above Chart Datum. Drying heights refer to areas such as mudbanks that are sometimes covered with water but will often be seen at low tide. A sounding of 6.5 metres, for example, is given as 6_5 whereas a drying height of 2.2 metres is given as $\underline{2}_2$. All tidal heights are measured from Chart Datum. To find the true depth of water at any point, you have to add the sounding to the height of tide (or subtract the drying height).

Exercise

Assume you are hoping to launch your boat into a tidal river you have never visited. The chart indicates a sounding of 0_3 metres in the middle of the channel and a drying height of $\underline{0}_8$ metres at the end of the slipway. So at first sight the launching site seems useless, so why is it there? If we look at the tide table it should provide the answer. At 10.00 hours on the day in question low water at this site is 1.4 metres while high water is 5 metres. Add the sounding (1.4 + 0'3) to the low water figure, and you find there is a minimum depth of 1.7 metres in the channel.

Deduct the drying height from the high water figure, and you discover that the end of the slip is 4.2 metres beneath the surface at high water. Since you do not want to wait around for this, you will need to find out when there will be about 1 metre of water at the end of the slip. (5.0 – 0.8=4.2)

Easy fix - Rule of 1/12ths
Find the range, divide it by 12 and hey presto (see Chapter on Tides on page 119). The chart and the tide tables have given you access to a completely new stretch of water.

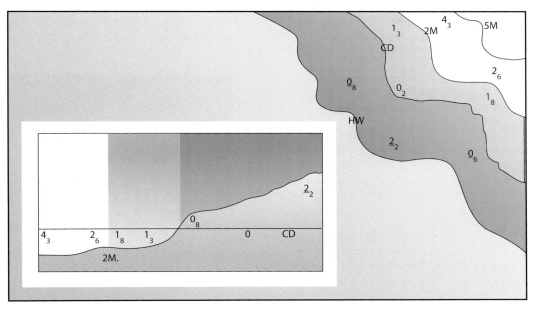

Typical cross section of a chart

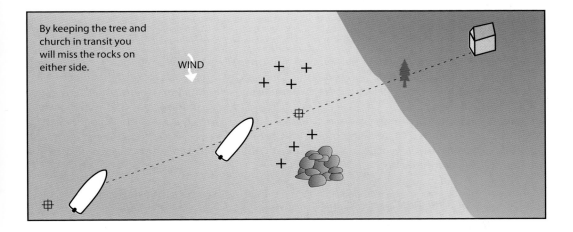

By keeping the tree and church in transit you will miss the rocks on either side.

WIND

Direction and compass

In enclosed waters you can often steer directly by visible landmarks or navigation marks. If you can identify these on the chart they provide ideal reference points. You can check the adjacent water for dangers and draw a clearing line on the chart that clears them all, passes through your visible reference point and aligns with the next visible feature. By keeping this transit aligned as you drive, the boat will stay on track regardless of wind and tide, and thus will keep you away from the rocks and sandbanks. We refer to this as pilotage

Compass rose

If you cannot find a visual alignment you will have to think in terms of a compass bearing.

Somewhere on the chart you will find a large circle printed with degrees. On some charts you will find an outer circle and an inner circle. The outer circle is the true compass rose with north aligned on the North Pole (and the vertical axis of the chart) longitudinal.

The inner circle is the magnetic compass rose with north aligned on magnetic north. This is usually different from the North Pole (and varies according to where you are in the world) but you need to know about it because it is the north indicated by your compass.

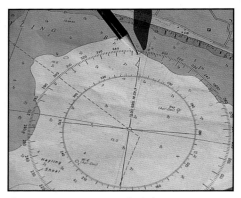

Compass rose on a nautical chart

Magnetic North Pole is a long way away from the true North Pole and is found somewhere above Queen Elizabeth Islands, Canada's northernmost islands.

Variation

Do you remember back at school placing a magnet under a piece of paper and sprinkling iron filings onto the paper? If so, do you recall the filings all being influenced by the magnetic field into a curved pattern? We referred to the pattern as lines of induction. The magnetic influence inside the Earth is similar, but because it is not under a flat piece of paper the lines of magnetic influence weave and curve their way across the face of the Earth. This magnetic influence can be measured and is referred to as variation, that is the difference between the magnetic north and the true north. In places this variation can be exactly the same as true north. Elsewhere it can be greater than 30° from true north.

The magnetic influence inside the Earth is on the move and scientists have decided that at some stage in the Earth's life the poles have been reversed.

If you now look at the compass rose on the chart you will see printed within it the variation and date and how much it is moving annually.

Exercise

In this example, I show a variation of 11°40' W 1979 decreasing about 4 minutes east annually. If you were in this area around the year 2000 you would have needed to adjust the variation from 11° 40' W. A 21 year alteration at 4 minutes annually represents 84 minutes, which is 1° and 24 minutes less than the 11° 40 minutes west shown in 1979. You would, therefore, have to turn the inner circle 1° 24 minutes to the right (clockwise) because it is now less of a variation west.

In reality, of course, you would throw the chart away or frame it and put it on the wall and purchase a new one where the date is as close as possible to the present day. Apart from the difference between magnetic north and true north, imagine all the other differences that have taken place with soundings, sandbanks, buoys and buoyage systems in the last 21 years. Old charts are dangerous, but it serves as a good example of the difference between magnetic compass and true north. It is also worth taking on board that all information relating to bearings on a chart is 'true'. It has to be 'true' because the magnetic variation is moving.

Bearings

If your chart has leading lights or transits you will see somewhere on this line a printed bearing. This bearing will be true. For example, the transit line up through Chichester Harbour onto Roman transit and onward to a clump of hills on the South Downs is 033° true.

Whatever chart you purchase of the area and whatever the date on that chart, the transit line will always be 033° true. If you were using a magnetic compass to move along the transit line and if the variation was 4° west you would be steering a compass bearing of 037° magnetic. With a westerly variation add it to the true and it will become the magnetic bearing for your ship's compass. If you are using a chart that shows the variation to be east then obviously do the opposite and subtract east from the true bearing to give you a magnetic heading.

Hence, the very well known expression when moving from true to magnetic: 'West is best, east is least'. Once you have that firmly fixed in your mind you can work magnetic back to true by doing a reversal of what you have just done.

Where you have the two compass roses, the magnetic and true, lay the parallel rules through the centre and you can easily see the difference in the headings. But, if you have only the outer circle, i.e. 'true', you will need to remember the information above and ensure that you correctly adjust the bearing. (On the example given here of 11° 40 minutes west you would actually be 22° to 23° off course if you subtracted it instead of adding it.)

Ship's compass and hand bearing

You may have two types of compass on board: a ship's compass and a hand-bearing compass. The ship's compass is mounted in front of the helm position, and you use it to steer by. If you want to steer directly east you turn the boat until the ship's compass indicates 90° and head off in that direction, watching the compass all the time. Modern electronic compasses are brilliant. Because they are computerised they can be automatically adjusted to take variation into consideration. Please refer to the handbook of the unit you are using and ensure you are conversant with it.

The hand-bearing compass is more interesting. You hold it in your hand, aim it at a visible mark, such as a buoy, and take a note of the bearing. This is useful when you are trying to stay on course and cannot find a visual alignment for your reference point.

Exercise

Draw a clearing line on the chart (see Direction and compass on page 110), avoiding all dangers and passing through the position of a conspicuous buoy if you have one. Or use two waypoints (see page 109).

Take your boat out to the first WP. If possible locate your next buoy on the water (make sure it is the right one). Take its bearing with your hand-bearing compass. Check this against the GPS; it should be close. Now forget the GPS and head towards the buoy rechecking its bearing at intervals with the hand-bearing compass. That way you should stay on course. Once you are on this course you may be able to align the buoy with a conspicuous object on shore, such as a tree or church. Keep both aligned as you head towards the buoy.

An instant transit like this saves a lot of rechecking with a compass and is more accurate. Having done this exercise, switch the GPS on and go back to the original WP. Commence moving in the direction of your second WP. Recheck the information that you have in the GPS and use it to retrace your course. I guarantee that the information you have in the GPS will not agree with the information that you have from your magnetic compass. If it has agreed exactly with the information then you are far too 'jammy' to be out boating. Remember, 'if at first you succeed be suspicious'.

Deviation

The ship's compass is influenced by surrounding parts of metal in the boat, the radio, the magnet in the speaker, the GPS if it is mounted close to the compass, a metal tin, or even a hand-bearing compass.

This is called deviation. It can be calculated and adjusted for. But in small boats this is seldom done. The magnetic ship's compass, therefore, gives you a general idea of your heading. The GPS, set up correctly, will be more accurate and take you to your target, but it is essential that you have both items on board.

A hand-bearing compass is also susceptible to deviation. Try standing by the car and take a reading. Now walk in a straight line away from the car towards your sighted object. Do not be surprised to see a thirty-degree swing away from the first reading. When on board the boat using a hand compass try taking a bearing near the radio speaker and then move away. Spectacles have been known to throw a compass off course.

Fluxgate compass

An electronic compass, however, can be swung through 360° and will automatically set itself for the deviation created by the boat. There is little point in attempting to plot a line across a chart to the nearest degree when the equipment on the boat is unable to complement your accuracy.

I have found in practice that the GPS is absolutely superb for travelling long distances across open water. However, buoy hopping up a channel in thick fog with a GPS when the buoys are only some 100 to 200 metres apart can cause a few problems. Parallel rules and magnetic bearings can prove to be much more accurate. Wave patterns, wind direction and the sideways movement of water will all move a boat off course.

Using a hand-bearing compass

Life before GPS

You should not rely entirely upon the GPS until you fully understand how you take compass bearings and transits to fix your waterborne position on to a chart. I suggest you find a quiet stretch of water and anchor up, or pick up a mooring buoy. This gives you the opportunity to spend plenty of time in trying to put into practice the following:

Fixing your position

Compass bearings and transits are used to fix your position as long as you are near charted objects, such as a buoy, chimney, church, etc. But what if the nearest buoy is some distance up an estuary, and you need to know where you are now so that you do not hit the mud? Aim the hand-bearing compass at the buoy and record the bearing.

Plotting aids

Locate this bearing on the magnetic compass rose on the chart and lay a rule across it (or adjust it for true and lay a line using your corrected true bearing). Find the buoy on the chart and draw a pencil line through the small circle at the base of the symbol parallel to the ruler. (If possible you should use parallel rules or a plotting device to ensure accuracy; this is not always practicable in a fast open boat, which is why I suggested that you anchor.) Now look around for another visible object that is marked on the chart, such as a buoy, beacon or building. Take a bearing and again draw a line. The two lines should cross at your position.

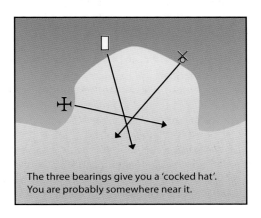

The three bearings give you a 'cocked hat'. You are probably somewhere near it.

11

Unfortunately, it is very hard to be accurate when you are doing this, so it is essential to take a bearing of yet another object as a check. If the third line/bearing crosses somewhere near the other two, forming a small triangle on the paper – referred to as a cocked hat – you can be reasonably sure of your position.

If the triangle is large, something is wrong. Try again, maybe by using a fourth object.

Transits
A transit can be more accurate than compass bearings, so if you can see, say a buoy and a lighthouse in direct alignment, draw a line through them on the chart and use this as one of your position lines.

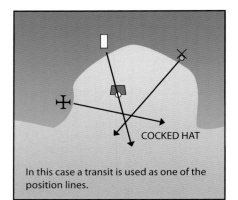

COCKED HAT

In this case a transit is used as one of the position lines.

However you use navigation marks, it is essential to identify them correctly. Use binoculars to spot buoys and check their features carefully against the information on the chart before you use them to fix your position.

Testing time
Having found your position on the chart and whilst remaining stationary, use three identifiable objects to obtain your latitude and longitude position (see pages 104-105). Write this down on a piece of paper. Now switch on the GPS and wait for it to locate its satellites. It will give you a latitude/longitude position of where you are. If the latitude and longitude position on the satellite navigator confirms accurately to the position that you have taken from the chart, you are certainly 'very very jammy'. You can see by the way I am writing that if it works out absolutely 'spot on' it is unusual. I am much happier when things are close because this is more like the real world.

Roman transit in Chichester–in line at 033ºT (from chart)

Limitations
Small powerboats are not really suitable for practising full navigational techniques, but if you want to venture out to sea you should know something about them anyway. It will only take approximately 20 minutes of time on the water for you to anchor, take the bearings, relay those bearings onto the chart and self-test your work. Never just switch on a GPS unit and assume that this is all you need to know. Just take on board the old expression, 'a little learning can be a dangerous thing'. Practise and test until it all becomes 'old hat'. By learning to be efficient with navigation your confidence will build, and you will become more relaxed and enjoy the sport much more. This, in turn, will mean that your family and friends will have more confidence in you, and you will become more of a pleasure to go out with.

Before we move on, just imagine the difficulty of carrying out this exercise at speed. It is impossible, so I use a flight plan where everything is organised before venturing out. (See section on fast navigation.)

We now have another section to look at before the story is complete.

11

Buoyage

The large-scale chart will give you details of all the buoys and beacons in the area. Many mark the channels needed by deep-drafted vessels, and may not concern you directly (always look at the chart to check). But they do make excellent reference points when you are out on the water, so it is well worth becoming familiar with them.

Starboard Hand Mark (SHM)

In harbours, estuaries and busy navigational routes, the deep water is marked either by posts or by floating navigation marks. These are colour-coded and of a characteristic shape. This shape is shown on the chart. Important navigation marks will be either named or numbered and again this will be shown on the chart.

Although many are floating in the current and moving around in the wind they are fairly accurate in their position: on the chart the little circle at the base of each symbol indicates its true position or best position. Floating buoys move around with the current and wind.

The colour and shape of a buoy indicates its function, but this varies according to where you are on the globe: Region A follows one convention and Region B another.

Buoyage in region 'A'

Region 'A' covers Europe, Africa, India, Australia and most of Asia.

Lateral marks

There are several different types of mark. The most familiar are probably the Lateral Marks that indicate channels. There are two of these: starboard-hand marks (green and cone-shaped) on the right-hand side of the channel when entering a harbour or estuary from the sea, and

Two cones pointing down; danger to north, southerly cardinal—keep south.

port-hand marks (red and can-shaped) on the left-hand side. With coastal channels the lateral marks are arranged according to the tidal stream, so if you are drifting on the flood tide (the rising tide) all the greens will be on the right and all the reds on the left. Where there is no tide they are arranged in the direction of the main navigation stream.

This left and right sometimes causes confusion. A useful memory jogger is, 'No red port wine left in the can'. Also, remember that 'port' has the same number of letters in the word as 'left'.

Lateral Marks change over as you move around an island, such as Anglesey, for example. If you travel up the Menai Straits, just outside Caernarfon there is a 'cardinal mark' (see Cardinal Marks) called 'Change', and it is at that point that the navigation marks change over from one side to the other.

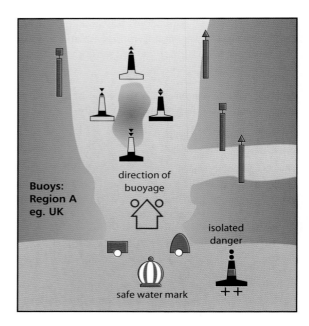

Buoys: Region A eg. UK — direction of buoyage — isolated danger — safe water mark

It is important to be able to recognise navigation marks by shape, because with bright sunshine behind them, or in poor visibility, their colour cannot be seen.

The most important navigation marks also have flashing lights that are also coloured and coded. They are marked on the chart in abbreviated form. For example, Fl G 3 10sec – flashing three green every ten seconds.

Special marks

Yellow marks, sometimes with a yellow cross on top, are Special Marks. They may be of any shape that is not easily confused with other marks and are used to indicate designated waterski areas, outer perimeter marks for swimmers, lanes for jet bikes and powerboats and so on. They are also used as racing marks for dinghies and yachts.

Cardinal marks

Yellow-and-black marks with two black cones on top are Cardinal Marks. They are named for the four cardinal points of the compass. Cardinal Marks are placed either north, south, east or west of a hazard, and you can tell the direction of the hazard by the pattern of the black cones, the arrangement of black-and-yellow stripes and the way the light flashes. Easy to remember: 2 cones up – north; 2 cones down – south; easterly is egg-shaped and westerly is 'W' on its side or a wine glass. To understand the flashing light pattern you need to know the sequence: northerly – continuously flashes very quick or quick; east – 3 o'clock flashes 3; south – 6 o'clock flashes 6; west – 9 o'clock flashes 9. All have pauses of darkness. The only special thing about the southerly is that it has a long flash after its 6 short flashes.

Isolated danger mark

A red-and-black mark with two black balls on top is an Isolated Danger Mark placed over a wreck or an isolated rock. You can pass on any side of this mark but please avoid the area of the mark itself. I have had a crew before now wanting to go really close so they could have a good look at one of these Isolated Danger Marks, and have had to advise them accordingly. They are not marks to investigate.

Safe water marks

You may also come across a Safe Water Mark, which is a buoy with vertical red-and-white stripes. This mark is quite important as it is often used at entrances to harbours and estuaries. The Safe Water Mark then becomes a line up buoy for other navigational marks. I have seen them used successfully for denoting a waterski area over mudflats. It is obviously more economical to place three Safe Water Marks than it is to place many Lateral Marks.

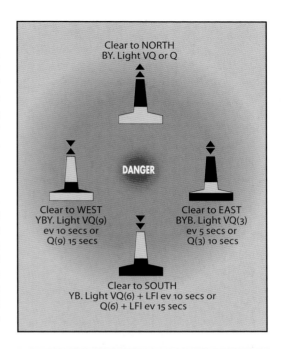

Clear to NORTH
BY. Light VQ or Q

DANGER

Clear to WEST
YBY. Light VQ(9)
ev 10 secs or
Q(9) 15 secs

Clear to EAST
BYB. Light VQ(3)
ev 5 secs or
Q(3) 10 secs

Clear to SOUTH
YB. Light VQ(6) + LFl ev 10 secs or
Q(6) + LFl ev 15 secs

Buoyage in region 'B'

Region B covers North, South and Central America, Canada, Japan, South Korea and the Philippines.

The main difference between the regions is in the Lateral Marks. Although the cone and can shapes are on the same sides as in Region A, the colours are reversed. Red is to starboard, while green is to port. Otherwise the system follows the same conventions as in Region A. Despite being British, the British Virgin Isles in the Caribbean use the American navigation system. I find it very difficult to get used to. It is much better if the sun is behind the navigation mark and the colour cannot be seen; then I just work to the shape.

The Special Marks are also yellow, with various top marks. They are used for anchorages and

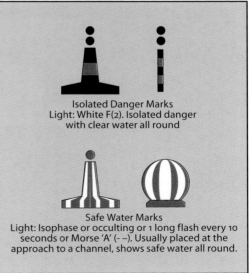

Isolated Danger Marks
Light: White F(2). Isolated danger
with clear water all round

Safe Water Marks
Light: Isophase or occulting or 1 long flash every 10
seconds or Morse 'A' (- –). Usually placed at the
approach to a channel, shows safe water all round.

11

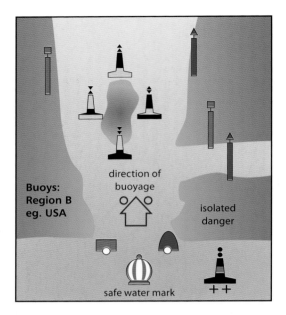

Buoys:
Region B
eg. USA

direction of
buoyage

isolated
danger

safe water mark

moorings, and may also warn of dangers such as firing ranges, pipelines, race courses, seaplane bases and areas where no through channels exist. Some mark waters where boats are prohibited, while others are for speed control, or give information. These have information panels set in them. These marks are used a lot in congested waters. When you are operating in any area other than the one that you know, do obtain up-to-date buoyage information as well as local tidal information. Speak to the people responsible for that area of water.

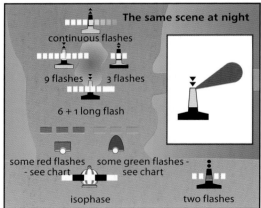

The same scene at night

continuous flashes

9 flashes   3 flashes

6 + 1 long flash

some red flashes - see chart   some green flashes - see chart

isophase   two flashes

Isolated Danger Marks
Light: White F(2).
Isolated danger with
clear water all round

Safe Water Marks
Light: Isophase or occulting or
1 long flash every 10 seconds
or Morse 'A' (- –). Usually
placed at the approach to a
channel, shows safe water all
round.

Not a navigational mark but indicating a special feature. Light (when fitted): Yellow. Any characteristic that
does not conflict with nav. marks.
May be any shape, topmark (if any):
Yellow X.

Emergency
marker
beacon

12 Theory of tides

Tide is the vertical rise and fall of a body of water. A tide does not go in and it does not go out! It is the tidal streams and currents that move horizontally.

The usual explanation for tidal behaviour, the Equilibrium Theory of Tides, was first proposed by Isaac Newton. According to this theory, the gravitational pull of the moon upon the Earth is responsible for two water bulges on the Earth's surface. There will be one bulge on the side of the Earth that faces the moon and the other bulge will be on the opposite side of the Earth furthest away from the moon. These lunar bulges draw the water, as in a tidal stream, towards the top of the bulge.

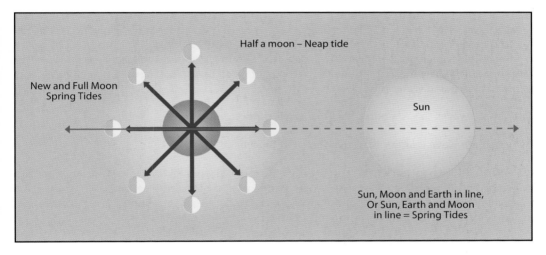

Spring tides

The sun causes similar, although much smaller solar bulges. When the sun and the moon are in line with the Earth (syzygy) their combined gravitational effect will cause the bulges to be larger than normal. This results in a larger, high tide. When it falls, the effect is a lower, low tide. This phenomenon is called a spring tide. When we subtract the difference in the predicted height of high water and low water for the day, we discover a large tidal range.

The fact that there are two bulges means that it is not important whether the moon, sun and Earth are in line on the same side, or on opposite sides. The result will be similar. The distance the moon is from the Earth reflects whether one spring tide will be of a different height to the next spring tide. This can be quickly seen when we scan over a 12-month period of tide predictions in a tide table.

Neap tides

When the moon and the sun are at right angles to the Earth then the lunar bulge will occur between the two solar bulges. This spreads the water more evenly over the surface of the Earth, reducing the size of the high tide and making the low tide less pronounced. In other words, the tide does not rise very high nor does it go down very far. Again, when subtracting the tide height differences, we find that the range is much less than the spring tides.

Theory vs. reality

The Equilibrium Theory allows for an easy understanding of the forces involved in the cause of tides. However, it does not explain how tides behave in reality.

The Equilibrium Theory does not work because the height of the tide caused by the moon alone would be about two-thirds of a metre high. For this 'wave' to follow the path of the moon it would have to travel 24,000 miles in 24 hours (the circumference of the Earth) at approximately 1,000mph. And the oceans would need to be over 12 miles deep! Thankfully this is not the case because a wave two-thirds of a metre high and travelling at 1,000mph would cause total devastation every 12 hours. Fortunately the water is unable to follow the pull of the moon because land masses act as breakwaters, and water is heavy and sluggish.

As tides are waves this is a good time to explain some common misconceptions:

Every seventh wave is larger than the ones that precede it. False.

The size of a wave depends on its source and whether it has combined with waves from a separate source. A distant storm may produce a swell with a periodic time of 9 seconds, whilst the local waves may have a periodic time of only 6 seconds. On the beach, starting with a big wave, we would get the following waves at the following times:

Each local wave rolls in every 6 seconds.

The storm wave comes along at every 9 seconds.

After 12 seconds we see the arrival of the next local wave.

At 18 seconds the local wave and the storm wave combine.

This means that we would get a large wave every four waves and this would only happen because the two waves arrive at the same time.

The wind blowing against the tide makes the waves larger and steeper. False. The wind is a little bit of a red herring. It is the direction of the waves with respect to the tidal flow that is important. The wind-generated waves are being bunched up because the tidal flow is attempting to slow their progress.

Predicting the tide

The phases of the moon work on a 28-day cycle and so do the tides. In 28 days (approximately) we get neaps, springs, neaps and springs again.

From this it might seem that you could predict the tides with some confidence, with a spring tide every other Tuesday, say. But it is not so easy. For one thing, the moon orbits the earth not once a day, but once every 24 hours and 50 minutes (on average). This means that High Water is roughly 50 minutes later each day. What's more, there is a two-day time lag between the moon phase and the corresponding tidal effect.

A Tide Gauge can either show the height of tide above Chart Datum or the depth of water over a feature such as a sill or drying area.

Add to this the influence of local topography, which creates different heights of tide at different points on the coast, plus the fact that the moon is constantly changing its orbiting speed and distance, and it becomes obvious that predicting the tide is no simple matter.

The answer is to buy a tide table, where it is all worked out for you. The table contains the time and height of high and low water for every day in the current year. Last year's table is no good, because all the figures change.

Although the tidal heights vary all along the coast, compiling a tide table for every stretch of water would be impracticable so obtain a tide table from your Harbour Master or Marina Manager. This should have been corrected for the location and apart from adjusting for GMT and BST you have no further adjustments to do.

Admiralty tide tables

Where this information is not readily to hand refer to the Tidal Almanac. The Almanac has information based on a Standard Port. If you are at this location no further adjustment is needed. The information is correct.

If, on the other hand, you are boating out of a Secondary Port the Almanac will refer you to the nearest Standard Port that has the same basic tidal characteristics as your own area - but there is usually a time difference and a height difference. This is indicated in a table, and you must either add or subtract the difference every time you use it.

Using the tide table

I am not going to discuss the finer points of time and height adjustment. I leave this to a shore-based course run by the RYA.

What I will do is to try and make it simple for you to understand the principles and therefore for you to be able to adjust time and heights close enough for your needs. Open up the Nautical Almanac for your local harbour and look at the tide table for the day in question and scan up and down either side of this date to find the Moon phase. A black circle is a new Moon and a white circle is a full Moon. Approximately two days after a symbol you will note the highest and lowest tides - Spring Tides. Half way between these symbols will be found the predictions for the Neap Tides.

JUNE	Time	m
16	0022	3.7
	0630	0.3
SU	1254	3.5
●	1855	0.6

GMT — or adjusted for BST?

Finding the time

Let us assume that you want to find the time of High Water on the afternoon of 16th June. The tide table entry is shown

The tide table entry is shown. What this means is that high water is at 0022 UT = 0122 BST and at 1254 UT = 1354 BST. Low water is at 0630 UT = 0730 BST and at 1855 UT = 1955 BST. The height in metres above chart datum (the depth shown on the chart) is shown in the right hand column.

Question: What time is high water on the afternoon of June 16?

Answer: 1354 BST (and it will have a depth of 3.5 m more than that shown on the chart.) Note that the times and heights may vary because of atmospheric pressure, storms etc.

If you discover that you are at a Secondary Port you will have to make adjustments to the time and to the height of tide.

Remember that the tidal height is the height of water to be added to the height given on the chart.

How to use the data

With Admiralty Tide Tables you will find a tidal curve associated with the Standard Port. Having made the adjustments [if needed], put the high water height along the top where it says High Water Heights in Metres and the low water height along the bottom where it says Low Water Heights in Metres. Join your two marks with a straight (green) line resulting in a slanting line.

12

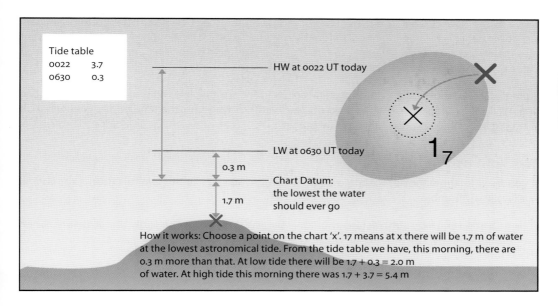

Tide table

| 0022 | 3.7 |
| 0630 | 0.3 |

HW at 0022 UT today

LW at 0630 UT today

0.3 m

Chart Datum:
the lowest the water
should ever go

1.7 m

1.7

How it works: Choose a point on the chart 'x'. 1.7 means at x there will be 1.7 m of water at the lowest astronomical tide. From the tide table we have, this morning, there are 0.3 m more than that. At low tide there will be 1.7 + 0.3 = 2.0 m of water. At high tide this morning there was 1.7 + 3.7 = 5.4 m

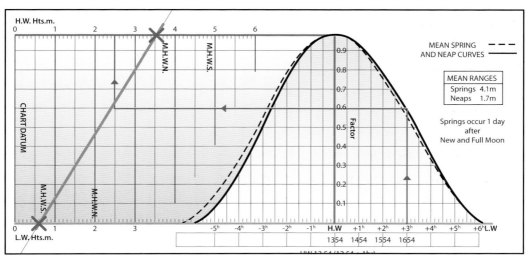

What is the height of tide at 1654 BST? 1654 = +3hrs after HW.
Height of tide is 2.5m. (Depth of water will be what is shown on the chart plus 2.5m)
What time in the afternoon is the height of tide 2.5m? Answer: 3hrs after HW ie 1654 BST. (Just follow the red line the other way!)

12

Move to the tidal curve and put the time of high water in the H.W. box at the bottom. You will see boxes either side showing hours before HW and hours after HW. Simply put the time you want into the correct box. Draw a vertical line (red) until it intersects either the Spring curve or the Neap curve (or somewhere in between).

From this intersection draw a horizontal line across to the slanting line. Where it crosses the slanting line move vertically up or down to read off the height of water for the time of day in question. It is simple and quick and just takes a little practice.

The rule of twelfths

If you need to know the approximate depth of water you can use the Twelfths Rule, a rough and ready rule of thumb.

First find the range by subtracting the Low Water height from the High Water height. Then divide the range by 12. The rate at which the tide falls (and rises) can be expressed in terms of this figure.

Example:
If the high water was 6.5 metres and the low water 0.5 metres the range would be 6.0 metres.
6.0 divided by 12 = 0.5
The Rule of Twelfths predicts that:
In the first hour the tide falls
1/12 = 0.5 metres
In the second hour the tide falls
2/12 = 1.0 metres
In the third hour the tide falls
3/12 = 1.5 metres
In the fourth hour the tide falls
3/12 = 1.5 metres
In the fifth hour the tide falls
2/12 = 1.0 metres
In the sixth hour the tide falls
1/12 = 0.5 metres
If you wanted to know the depth of water four hours after High Water, add the hours up like this:

First hour:	0.5 metres
Second hour:	1.0 metres
Third hour:	1.5 metres
Fourth hour	1.5 metres
Total	4.5 metres

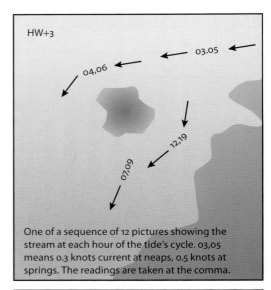

One of a sequence of 12 pictures showing the stream at each hour of the tide's cycle. 03,05 means 0.3 knots current at neaps, 0.5 knots at springs. The readings are taken at the comma.

Not all tides rise and fall in 6 hours (plus a few minutes). The Solent area of the UK rises in 7 hours and falls in 5-therefore, use the Almanac.

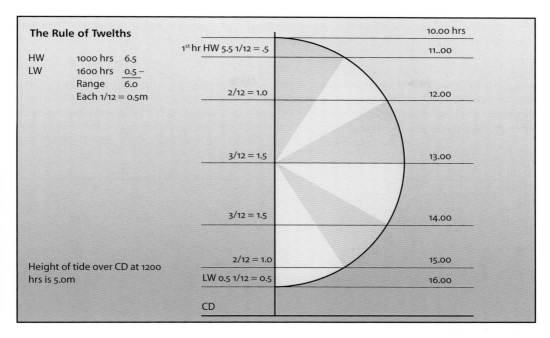

The Rule of Twelths

HW	1000 hrs	6.5
LW	1600 hrs	0.5 –
	Range	6.0
	Each 1/12 = 0.5m	

1st hr HW 5.5 1/12 = .5

2/12 = 1.0

3/12 = 1.5

3/12 = 1.5

Height of tide over CD at 1200 hrs is 5.0m

2/12 = 1.0

LW 0.5 1/12 = 0.5

CD

10.00 hrs
11..00
12.00
13.00
14.00
15.00
16.00

12

You can then deduct this figure from the height of High Water: 6.5 metres - 4.5 metres = 2.0 metres above the figure on the chart. Note that the figures used here are the figures for the Standard Port. If you are operating some way down the coast you will need to modify these before you start the calculation (and correct them for local time).

Look at it from another angle: at High Water the tide has reached its maximum height and during the next hour it falls slowly, then speeds up during the second hour. It falls fastest during the third and fourth hours, before slowing down to stop at Low Water.

It follows the same pattern as it rises. Naturally the actual rate of fall will depend on how far it is going to drop: during a spring tide it will fall much faster than during a neap. It is important to appreciate that the rule of twelfths indicates a rise and fall of a body of water.

Tidal streams

As tide rises and falls, so the body of water moves back and forth. Tidal streams are the horizontal movement of water, flooding as the tide rises and ebbing as it goes out. Referring to the Twelfths Rule, it is easy to imagine that the movement at High Water is virtually nil. Sadly, the vertical movement of water is not necessarily related to horizontal movement. It is quite possible to have several knots of current at high tide, for example. The Almanac has pictures showing the stream at each hour of the 12-hour cycle. Obviously the tidal stream will move faster during a spring tide than a neap tide, and that's why there are two figures on each arrow.

The chart has tidal diamonds, with a key located on an uncluttered part of the chart. They also give the streams' strength and direction at various states of the tide.

Apart from the obvious problem of fighting a strong tidal stream with inadequate power, you can also get into trouble where a large body of moving water is squeezing through a narrow channel or over a shallow area. As the speed of water increases it swirls into whirlpools and stopper waves; in some places the water appears to boil as if it were in a cauldron. Such tide rips and overfalls often occur close to headlands, estuaries and channels, and are shown on the charts. If the water is deep enough they can be negotiated at the right state of the tide (usually slack water), but they are best avoided.

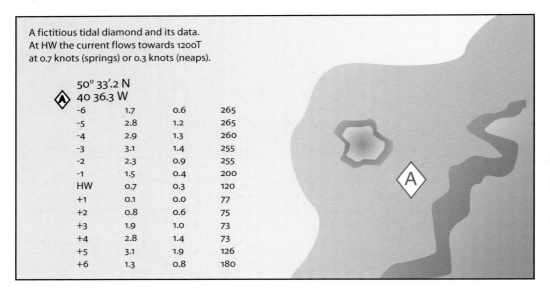

A fictitious tidal diamond and its data.
At HW the current flows towards 120oT
at 0.7 knots (springs) or 0.3 knots (neaps).

50° 33'.2 N
40 36.3 W

-6	1.7	0.6	265
-5	2.8	1.2	265
-4	2.9	1.3	260
-3	3.1	1.4	255
-2	2.3	0.9	255
-1	1.5	0.4	200
HW	0.7	0.3	120
+1	0.1	0.0	77
+2	0.8	0.6	75
+3	1.9	1.0	73
+4	2.8	1.4	73
+5	3.1	1.9	126
+6	1.3	0.8	180

Steering in a cross-tide

When you are travelling at high speed across a tidal stream your sideways drift is minimal, but if you are motoring at slow displacement speed the current will push you off course. Simply aiming for your goal is no help: you will still drift sideways and finish up approaching from the wrong angle. The best approach is to align your goal visually with something behind it, such as a headland or tree, and keep them aligned as you travel. This *transit* will keep you on track regardless of any tidal effects.

Passage planning and fast cruising

Once you understand tides, charts and navigation marks you can use this knowledge to fix your position in inshore waters and work out a course to steer that avoids danger and delivers you swiftly and safely to your destination.

Most open-water navigation methods are beyond the resources of the small sportsboat owner, but a few basic pilotage techniques (employed inshore where there are plenty of buoys and landmarks) are well worth mastering. Once you move up in size to 6.5 metres or more anything is possible. RIBs and sportsboats of this length often make long passages across open sea.

Planning a cruise for a day or even longer

The golden rule with such a trip is, NEVER ATTEMPT IT ALONE. A fully-equipped sports-boat is still vulnerable. Find some friends who would like to venture further afield in their boat, or contact your club committee members and ask them to organise a day or weekend trip. Pool your resources.

Preparation

When you have made up your party, get together and pore over all the charts, tide tables and harbour information. For your first long trip, avoid being too ambitious. Work on the principle of small hops. Remember to match the speed and distance to the size of the smallest boat.

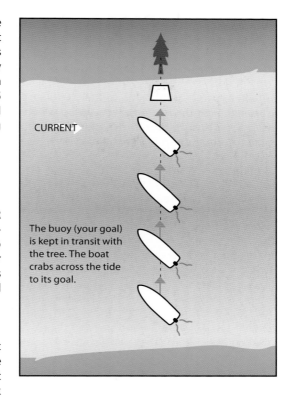

CURRENT

The buoy (your goal) is kept in transit with the tree. The boat crabs across the tide to its goal.

If the conditions allow you to travel at 20 knots, then in theory you will take one hour to travel 20 nautical miles. In practice, with wind and tide, it may well take longer. Check the forecast wind direction and strength and try to plan so that you are travelling into the wind on the outward leg of the journey. This is the wetter and colder route. If the conditions worsen and you are forced to return home, you will run down-wind and should have a reasonably soft, dry and warm return passage down the backs of the waves.Consider, in particular:

- Have we enough fuel? Many lifeboats are launched simply because people ran out of juice.

- Is your chart waterproof, or in a water-proof case? Have you a spare?

- On the chart draw your route. For each leg, write alongside the magnetic bearing (so you can steer on the compass) and the distance.

- Mark on the chart danger areas such as rocks, and draw on clearing bearings. Check which way the tide is going, and the depth of water at any critical point e.g. over shallow patches and at your landing places.

Bolt holes

Use the chart to check for bolt-holes - safe ports where you can drive for cover if the conditions deteriorate. You need to know the whereabouts of such places and how to enter them in safety. (One of you might even be under tow with an engine down.)

Obtain a current **pilot book** of the coastline. They hold a fantastic amount of information plus plans and sketch maps, waypoints (WPs), weather, radio beacons, major lights, coast radio stations, navigable distances, key to symbols, photographs of entrances and headlands. The whole of this section is about the 5 Ps - Preparation Prevents Pretty Poor Performance.

Keep people informed

Radio communication between the craft is essential: consider a ship-to-ship channel.

Either the Coastguard or the family need to know the proposed route of your journey. Give them your ETA (estimated time of arrival) and how much time to allow before calling the rescue agencies if you do not appear.

They will need to know the type of craft they are looking for, its name, colour, size and the number of people on board. They will also ask for details of equipment carried and the proposed route of the journey. The completion of Coastguard Form CG66 means that they will know exactly what they are looking for. This remains valid for three years (and is free).

One member of the party should contact the person in charge at your proposed destination: the marina controller or harbourmaster. This ensures that you are made welcome and that there is sufficient room for your group to moor up or berth.

Ensure that you can refuel and the correct grade of fuel for your engine is available. (Alternatively, you may be able to carry all your fuel with you.) Decide on the maximum wind strength for your smallest craft. Do not be tempted to take a friend's boat if it is unsuitable. You may decide to drop it and double up on another boat. Flexibility is the key to success.

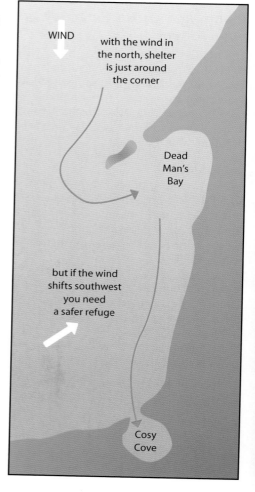

WIND

with the wind in the north, shelter is just around the corner

Dead Man's Bay

but if the wind shifts southwest you need a safer refuge

Cosy Cove

12

Weather
Having planned a coastal hop in great detail, the most difficult decision is whether to cancel the venture because of threatened adverse weather conditions. A full-blown gale will not present a problem since everyone will be in agreement to give up the whole idea. The difficulty arises when there is a high wind predicted, but the day dawns bright and sunny with a light breeze blowing. The best advice here is: if in doubt, don't go to sea. Have an alternative plan whereby you can enjoy each other's company on dry land.

If the waves are lumpy with a strong wind it will always look more inviting in sunshine than if it is raining. Sunshine sometimes does no one any favours when deciding on a trip.

Wind Strengths
As you know Force 8 is a gale on the Beaufort (wind strength) Scale. This information is required for ships. You should consider a Force 5 to Force 6 (17 knots - 27 knots) as a sportsboat's gale, and in certain cases a Force 3 (7 -10 knots) with wind-over-tide is sufficient to sink a small boat. (see page 9)

Clothing and protection
In a RIB I recommend a drysuit over thermals. In a conventional sportsboat I would use a good quality yachtsman's two-piece or one-piece suit offering full weather protection, over the top of several layers of loose warm clothing. Always take spare warm clothes and towels stowed in a waterproof kitbag. Use glasses or goggles for eye protection.

Refreshment – no alcohol
Eat well before embarking on a journey but stay clear of alcohol, which lowers your resistance to exposure. It also impairs your ability to make correct decisions.

Canadian research has proved beyond doubt that impairment of judgement on the water is caused by only a third of the amount of alcohol that causes impairment on the road. Follow their slogan "Don't booze and cruise".

Ready-prepared food
Carry hot drinks or soup in a crush-proof thermos. Pack a supply of sandwiches, fresh fruit, crisps, chocolate and fresh water, together with plastic cups and spoons. Try cans of stew that automatically heat the contents when needed. All food and drink needs to be easily available and digestible in small quantities.When it is very rough the crew cannot move about to reach for food and drink, it has to be ready to hand.

Personally prepared
Pay a visit to the toilet before climbing into your wetsuit/drysuit. It will be difficult to relieve yourself in a fast open sportsboat when you are wearing several layers of clothing. Consider the ladies' comfort as well, otherwise the men will be doing all the journeys on their own.

12

Ready for the 'off'

Check the weather and put on your lifejacket. Run up the engines and make sure they are working and you are ready to go. Check all navigation equipment, plus back-up. Ensure there is a secondary supply of electric power.

The journey

Record in the log the time you set off, fuel quantity and number of people on board. Who has been informed of the journey?

Move out into deeper water and hug the coast, following your predetermined route by checking your position with known navigation marks and landmarks. Use the GPS and your pre-determined flight plan and each time you stop, update the log.

You will be unable to take efficient bearings and fixes when travelling fast. You will have to rely on visual reference with GPS support.

- Don't motor too close behind other boats. Travel in echelon formation, like geese in flight.

- Keep an eye on the direction from which the weather is approaching.

- Do adopt a speed that is comfortable for your boat and the other craft travelling with you. Maintain visual contact with them at all times.

- Have definite hold points along the way where the lead boat stops and waits for the rest of the fleet to catch up.

- Check that everyone's engine is functioning properly and more importantly that everyone is enjoying the experience. Do they all know what they are doing and where they are going?

You experience a wonderful euphoria on completing a successful trip. This makes all the planning and organisation worthwhile. If you cover all the angles everything should go smoothly and you will learn a lot. Have a good day!

10 Knots	3 Minutes	1,000 Yards	0.5 Nautical Mile
20 Knots	3 Minutes	2,000 Yards	1 Nautical Mile
40 Knots	3 Minutes	4,000 Yards	2 Nautical Miles

Can you be seen by radar?

The answer is a big resounding NO because the engine is low down and the boat is non-metallic. For this reason you need to fit a radar reflector - a specially shaped arrangement of reflecting surfaces that gives a set size of return back to the radar set. There are different types of reflectors but whichever you choose mount it as high as possible with the best 360 degree clear view. Mount the radar reflector well away from your radar scanner or you will see yourself. Make sure there is no mast or superstructure in the way, as this will cause blind spots.

Chest compression

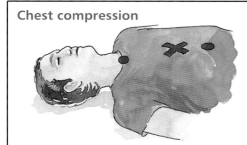

Identify a point 2/3 down the breast bone.

Recovery position

The safest posture for an unconscious casualty who is breathing is the recovery position. This position will maintain an open airway. When a casualty begins to regain consciousness they often vomit, in order to clear their own airway. In this position, the casualty's tongue cannot block the airway and their head is slightly lower than the rest of the body so that any fluid in the mouth can drain away, reducing the risk of inhalation.

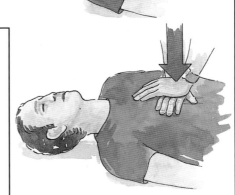

Rock forward with stiff arms. Relax. Pepeat 100 times per minute.

You will have to modify the position for certain injuries or the environment that the casualty is in. Obviously, it is not possible to place a casualty in the recovery position if they are still in the water, therefore you must get them into a boat. Once in the boat it is advisable to align the casualty's head towards the stern with their feet to the bow. This means that when the boat is moving the casualty's head will be lower than their feet, which aids drainage.

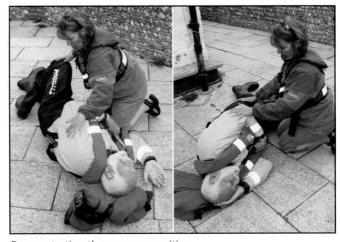

Demonstrating the recovery position

13

Bleeding

If the casualty is wet the water will spread the blood and make the injury look worse than it really is. Remember this and try not to look too alarmed. For obviously serious wounds call for medical aid, via the radio, if you are on a boat.

With a major wound the priority is to stop profuse bleeding. Initially this can be achieved by direct pressure on the wound and by elevating it above the heart if possible. You should think about the position of the casualty. Once bleeding is under control, apply a clean, dry, sterile dressing if you have one; if not use anything handy.

CPR in a cramped position

With a minor wound your priority is to prevent infection. If the wound is dirty, clean it with fresh water (a safety boat should carry a supply of tap water) and then apply a dressing pad and secure it in place.

If the wound has an object embedded in it DO NOT exert pressure directly over the object or remove it, as this will make the situation worse. If you need to apply pressure to control bleeding, press onto the side of the object to seal up the wound. Bandage around the injury not over the top.

When bleeding is severe and cannot be controlled by direct pressure it will be necessary to apply indirect pressure at a site remote from the injury (pressure point). This procedure is only effective for wounds on an arm or leg. Pressure points are located at the top of each arm on the inner side and at the top of the leg near the centre of the groin crease. Pressure applied here must not be held for more than 10 minutes. The pressure must be released slowly to allow blood to circulate around the limb to reduce tissue damage and prevent gangrene.

Shock

Shock is dangerous in its own right – people can die from shock if it is not recognised and treated accordingly. Any injury will have a degree of shock associated with it, so treat all casualties for its effects.

Shock occurs due to a lack of oxygen in the body tissues. Its effect is to increase the body's demand on its blood supply for oxygen. This condition can be brought on by loss of body fluid such as blood, serum from burns or continuous vomiting or diarrhoea. As the brain demands more oxygen the pulse will become rapid and weak, whilst breathing will become fast and shallow. Various parts of the body will shut down so that the remaining oxygen can be sent to the vital organs. As oxygen levels fall these organs will become affected. The casualty will look pale and be cold and clammy to the touch as blood is concentrated at the core of the body and brain.

The condition will be made worse by pain, stress and unnecessary movement.

External bleeding

The safest and surest way of stopping bleeding is by direct pressure on the site of the bleeding.

Direct pressure

1 Hold the edges of the wound together and apply pressure to the wound with your fingers.

2 Place a clean dressing over the wound, then press directly onto the dressing.

3 Cover the dressing with a pad. If the bleeding continues add more padding but do not disturb the first dressing. Continue to apply pressure to the pad.

Apply an elastic adhesive bandage tightly over the pad. If the bleeding is from a limb continue the elastic bandage right round the limb, then check the casualty's fingers and toes to make sure that the circulation has not been stopped completely. They must remain pink and not become white or blue. If they do, take off the bandage and reapply it less tightly.

This casualty needs an improved blood supply to the brain, heart and lungs. Treatment should therefore consist of:

- Treating the cause.
- Laying the casualty down and raising the legs to encourage blood flow to the brain (injuries permitting).
- Wrapping the casualty up to keep them warm and conserve body heat; do not use direct localised heat.
- Loosening any tight clothing to ease breathing.
- Giving plenty of reassurance – speak calmly, look cheerful. It is important that the casualty has faith in your ability to help.
- Protecting them from the wind and spray.
- Moistening their lips if they complain of thirst, but DO NOT GIVE DRINKS, FOOD, ALCOHOL OR STIMULANTS.
- Do not let the casualty smoke; they need all the oxygen they can get.
- Obtaining medical help.
- Rescue can be a traumatic business for all concerned. Be aware of all those involved and watch for their reactions; they may need treatment later.

13

Hypothermia

The waters around Britain are cold even in the height of summer. Sea temperatures can range from 32° to 68° F (0° C to 20° C); inland water and deep water can be colder still. Bodies in cold water cool 30 times faster than those in dry air. Moving air has a great cooling effect – the 'wind chill factor'.

The human body has a built-in thermostat that maintains its temperature at 98.6° F (37° C). An increase or decrease of only a few degrees at the body core can be fatal. In cold conditions the thermostat conserves heat by closing down the supply of warm blood to the extremities; these may go cold and numb as a result. This action is usually enough to keep the core temperature above 95° F (35° C), but if not the casualty's body heat will gradually ebb away until they die. This is a very real possibility when someone has been in the water for some time or has been left wet and exposed to the wind.

The symptoms of hypothermia will follow this pattern:

1   complaints of feeling cold;
2   apathy, irrational behaviour;
3   skin abnormally cold, pale and dry;
4   shivering violently;
5   shivering may stop, or it may continue to the point of death.
6   no muscle coordination;
7   slurred speech;
8   comprehension dulled;
9   pulse and respiration slow down;
10 unconsciousness and death.

Your aims are to prevent further heat loss, warm the casualty and seek medical aid.

Usually, if the casualty is still shivering they will probably be fine as long as you keep them warm (see exception above). If they have gone beyond that, take them ashore immediately. On the way, treat as follows:

■   Isolate the casualty from the elements using an exposure bag, thermal blanket or even a bin liner.

■   Insulate the casualty and warm them up by covering their body, head and neck, but not their face. Do not remove wet clothing if you are out in an open boat – just add extra clothes. You should have these onboard a safety boat. Consider asking a warm person to climb into the bag with the casualty.

■   If unconscious, place the casualty in the recovery position. Monitor their airway, breathing and circulation carefully – be prepared to resuscitate and call for assistance (see previous sections).

- If conscious, offer a warm drink (if you have one). NOT ALCOHOL.

- Do not encourage exercise and do not rub or massage the casualty as this will only encourage warm blood away from the body core, where it is needed. Similarly, if you have access to a warm bath on shore, do not simply dump them in it; keep arms and legs out of the warm water to retain the warm blood at the body core. If using a shower, do not let them stand. Sit them down and do not leave them alone.

13

Survival times

Survival time in cold water depend on the water temperature, air temperature, the casualty's age, weight, health and fitness, and the efficiency of their protective clothing. Survival time will be reduced if they have been drinking alcohol.

The following chart shows approximate survival times with water temperature:

Water Temperature		Survival
F° (°C)		
59	(15)	3 hours
50	(10)	2 hours
41	(5)	90 minutes
32	(0)	2–3 minutes

This section is not intended to cover all First Aid eventualities you might come across whilst powerboating. As in many other situations, prevention is better than cure. By increasing your awareness of health and safety issues the number of potential accidents can be reduced. Some accidents are just that, accidents, and training will increase your confidence in being able to cope with them.

14 Engine and trailer troubleshooting

A handpull start on an outboard engine should be successful by the third attempt. If it isn't then something is amiss. Don't keep on: continual pulling for ten minutes can cause the breakdown of the ignition unit. Leave it alone and go through the following checklist.

Fuel

- Have you any fuel?
- Is it turned on?
- Has the bulb in the fuel line been primed? (You should feel a resistance when it is squeezed.)
- Is it connected from the petrol tank through to the engine?
- Has the top cap of the fuel tank been released to allow air into the tank when the fuel is taken out?
- Is the kill switch fitted? The engine will not - or should not - start without it
- Is the fast idle lever or throttle control in the correct start-up position? If it is in the 'engaged gear' position the ignition circuit is not live and it will not start.

Electric start

A cold engine will need choke until it fires.

If the engine has an ignition key you may need to push it in as you turn it to bring in the automatic choke. Other systems may be fitted with a separate switch for the choke. Electronic fuel ignition systems will have an automatic choke.

As soon as the engine fires, take off the choke control and it should run fast. Set the tick-over at about 1500 rpm and warm up for three minutes.

If you have checked the choke and the engine still won't go, check the plugs.

Plugs

Remove the plugs (make sure you have a plug spanner in your tool kit) and if it's a two-stroke system check them for oil. Sniff them: they should smell of petrol. Clean the plugs and check the ignition gap, or replace them with new ones.

If the engine still doesn't fire you will have to get it looked at by a qualified engineer.

Cooling system

Even if the engine starts, this does not mean that all is well. If the cooling system isn't working, the engine will run perfectly for a while, then overheat and seize up. Modern engines are electronically controlled and will sound warning buzzers or close down until cool.

On an outboard, the cylinder block is cooled by water pumped up from an inlet in the lower leg assembly, under the cavitation plate. Because the pump's impeller uses water as its lubricant, never run an outboard engine out of the water unless water is supplied to the inlet through a muff connected to a hosepipe.

14

When the engine is ticking over there should be a jet of water (emerging from somewhere below the engine cover) as an indication that all is well. This outlet is a narrow tube that can easily become blocked: clear it by pushing a thin wire up inside the tube to clear it. If this fails lift off the hood - you should find a plastic grommet where the tube exits through the casing. Remove the grommet with a pair of pliers and check that it is clear. Before replacing the tube and engine hood, restart the engine. Water should shoot out of the rubber tube. If not close down the engine and have it serviced, or you risk destroying it. Much the same goes for inboard engines that are cooled by external water. Check your engine manual.

Mud

Do not operate the drive leg through mud, because it will be pumped around the engine through the cooling water passages and will set solid. Hot spots will arise inside the engine and metal will crack. Note that this mud blockage is unlikely to affect the exiting water jet.

Propeller and gearbox

If the engine is running well but you are getting no propulsion, there may be a fault with the propeller or gearbox. Try the following checks and tests.

- Switch off the engine and check the propeller. It is held in place by a washer, lock nut and split pin. If this lock nut is not secured correctly, the propeller can fall off. Has it? If so, do you carry a spare lock nut, split pin and propeller?

- Turn off the engine and remove the kill cord. If you can turn the propeller on the shaft by hand when the engine is in gear, check the shear pin or rubber compression bush. The shear pin is a small, soft metal pin, which snaps if something jams the propeller. Small engines up to 4 hp are usually fitted with a shear pin, while modern, larger engines are generally fitted with a rubber compression bush which is designed to slip if the propeller jams thus preventing damage to the gearbox.

- Check the gear-change mechanism. This can work loose and become disconnected from the gearbox, in which case moving the gearlever back and forth will have no effect.

- With the engine off (remove the kill cord) move the gear lever into forward or reverse gear. Apply gentle pressure to the propeller. This should be locked and unable to move in one direction. If it does move, and feels rough and lumpy - a grinding feel - check the gearbox for internal damage.

14

(Do not exert so much pressure on the propeller that it turns when in gear. Engines have been known to fire up and remove a hand.)

A floating spanner is really useful; heavy crew on the bow to lift the stern

Changing propellers

If you damage your propeller you will have to remove it from the engine and replace it. This is a fairly simple operation which can sometimes be carried out at sea using a pair of pliers, screwdriver, spanner, hammer and block of wood - assuming you carry a spare propeller!

Make sure you do. Find a couple of heavy crew to stand on the bow to lift the stern. A spanner that floats is a useful tool. Use a bag around the propeller and work inside it. Anything dropped will end up in the bag.

Here's how you do it.

1   Take a look at the locking nut. If it is a 'castle' nut held in place by a split pin, squeeze the splayed ends of the pin together with pliers and withdraw it.

2   If the nut is locked in place by a tab washer, lever the tabs out of their grooves with a screwdriver. Use a piece of wood to protect the anti-cavitation ring of the propeller. (This is the outer ring of metal.)

3   When all the locking tabs are released (or the split pin has been removed) undo the nut with a spanner. Wedge the propeller against the cavitation plate with the block of wood to stop it rotating.

4   If the shaft is regularly greased the propeller should now come off. If not, hold your block of wood behind the propeller and hit the wood with a hammer until the propeller comes free. Never strike the propeller directly.

5   Take the propeller off, being careful not to lose the thrust ring - usually a loose ring that looks like a washer which prevents the propeller from screwing itself through the gearbox.

6   Grease the shaft with recommended biodegradable grease. Reverse the sequence to refit the propeller.

7   Propellers are also removed for security reasons, since they are a favourite target for thieves. If you have to leave your boat unattended in the boat park it makes sense to remove the propeller before someone else does.

Bleeding a diesel

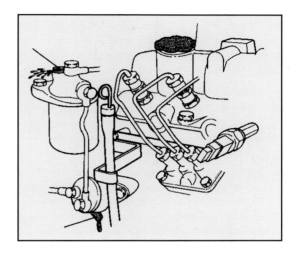

You should know how to remove air from a diesel fuel system, because you might need to do it at sea.

1   The 'bleeding points' vary and will be shown in the engine manual. Identify the bleed screw and slacken it off. Normally this is on the fine filter housing (A).

2   Work the hand priming lever on the fuel lift pump (B).

3   If the fuel coming from the vent contains bubbles, there is probably air in the system. Continue pumping until clear fuel flows out with no bubbles. Tighten the screw while continuing to work the lift pump.

4   If no fuel comes from the vent the primary fuel filter (C) may be blocked. Close the fuel cock at the tank. Clean out the filter, replace the element, open the fuel cock, then complete bleeding as in step 3.

5   If, after replacing the pre-filter, fuel still does not flow replace the element in the fine filter (D) and repeat the operation.

6   If clear fuel comes from the vent but, after tightening the vent, the engine still does not start slacken the high pressure line to one injector, and turn over the engine until fuel flows without bubbles.

In summary, there are two basic requirements: Fuel must be able to pass freely through both filters. The fuel system must be completely free of air.

Recovering a drowned petrol engine

If your engine comes off the boat, or is swamped, the circumstances surrounding the accident will determine whether it will restart. Generally speaking, if the engine was running at speed when immersed, water will have been taken into the cylinder head through the carburettor. Unlike air which compresses, water does not reduce its volume under pressure, and the engine will seize up. However, if you are able to recover the engine from the water quickly after a swamping, it is worth trying the following.

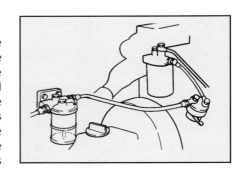

1   Check that the fuel has not been contaminated by the water.

2   Remove the drain plugs on each of the carburettors and prime the fuel system until all the water and dirt is removed, leaving neat petrol flowing out. Replace the drain plugs on the carburettors.

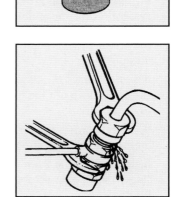

3   Remove all spark plugs and turn the engine over. There should be minimal resistance and the engine should turn over easily. At this point you will know whether there is a chance of the engine restarting. If a large quantity of water was taken into the cylinders at speed, the engine will have seized and will not turn. It will need to be rebuilt.

4   If the engine turns, it should push any water and dirt out of the cylinders' plug holes.

5   Give a quick squirt of water displacement oil into each pot.

6   Replace the plugs. Check that the fuel system is primed.

7   Apply water displacement oil liberally over the entire engine.

8   Return to the normal starting procedure and re-start the engine.

Well, were you lucky?

Maintenance and storage

The best way to deal with problems is to avoid them. Ensure that you maintain the boat well and store it properly at the end of the season. But the most basic element of maintenance is the daily routine after recovering the boat from the water.

Wash down

Use fresh water to wash down the hull and trailer. Then connect the engine muff to the hosepipe, attach it to the cooling water inlet and turn on the tap. Fire up the engine. Hopefully all the salt water, sand and mud will be washed out of the cooling system. With 2-stroke outboards, remove the fuel line and allow the engine to run dry. This prevents the oil residue being left in the carburettors when the petrol evaporates. Over a period of weeks this oil can clog the jets and make the engine difficult to start.

If you follow this routine religiously it should keep the engine in good shape all season. However, there is more to maintenance than simply flushing out the system after every trip. New engines can have a hosepipe adapter for flushing.

14

Basic care of outboard engines

The whole engine needs to be kept clean and dry. WD40 is often used for displacing water from the electrics and moving parts, but use it sparingly because it hardens as it dries and can build up a yellow skin over the engine surface causing the high-power electrical current to leak away. Better to use the water-displacement oil sold for marine engines which does the same job as WD40, but leaves a thin film of oil which does not dry.

Periodically wash down the whole engine using engine de-greasing gunk followed by a solution of a soap-based washing-up liquid. This also leaves a very thin oily film behind when it dries.

Paintwork
Look after the engine paintwork. Wash it down with fresh water and a soap-based washing-up liquid, and retouch any scars with zinc chromate paint. The engine and covers are often made of aluminium, and this has an electrolytic action when chipped and exposed to salt water which will eventually corrode the whole unit.

Grease
Use the grease specified by manufacturers. This is bio-degradable and won't react with salt water.

Gearbox oil
The gearbox has its own oil, drain plug and filler plug. Always use the oil recommended by the manufacturer and change as necessary. When changing, note whether it looks 'milky'. If it does, this can mean that salt water has seeped in through a loose seal and the gearbox needs servicing. This is sometimes caused by a fishing line tightly wrapped around the back of the propeller: drop off the prop and check. You will also find the oil milky if the lower leg has been cooked from cavitation/ventilation.

Two-stroke oil
Two-stroke engines need oil mixed with the fuel to lubricate the engine. Use the recommended oil and mix it to the correct proportions. Large engines usually work on a 50:1 mix of fuel to oil. With many engines you simply fill an oil reservoir, and the engine mixes it automatically. Do not use the two-stroke oil used for motorbikes and mowing machines, since it does not burn at the correct temperature and can dramatically reduce the life of the engine.

Most two-stroke engines will operate on low-octane or unleaded fuel. Check the octane rating of the fuel against the engine specifications.

Fuel system

Cleanliness of the fuel system is essential. Prevent sand, dirt and water from entering the fuel tank. Keep fuel lines clean and in good order. Use an in-line fuel filter to remove water. If you suspect water in the system use a recommended petrol additive to break it down into minute manageable particles.

Basic care of inboard engines

Similar treatment is recommended for inboard engines. De-gunk and wash down with a soap-based washing-up liquid. Use a watering-can, and pump out the bilge. Dry the engine and spray it with water-displacement oil.

Petrol (gasoline)

Petrol inboards are similar to car engines and require similar servicing.

- Ensure that the petrol filters are changed regularly.
- Check that the engine is always pumping cooling water.
- Check oil levels.
- If a heat exchanger is fitted check the water level and remember to add anti-freeze for the winter (not necessary in warm climates). Make sure the anti-freeze is suitable for an aluminium engine head and heat exchanger.

Diesel

- Change the filters on the fuel line regularly to remove dirt. There should be at least two filters on the system.
- Check the water separator in the fuel line. Water is heavier than diesel and collects in a bowl at the bottom near a drain-off tap or screw. This needs to be released from time to time to remove the water.
- Check the level of the engine oil, and change it at the recommended intervals.
- Check the level of the gearbox oil, and change it at the recommended intervals. Always use the oil specified by the manufacturer.
- Check that the engine is pumping cooling water.
- Check the water level in the heat-exchanger unit (if fitted) and make sure it contains an anti-freeze solution of the right type.

Storage (winterisation) of outboards

Have the engine fully serviced at the end of the season.

The fuel system should be stripped down completely, cleaned, rebuilt and tested. Then drain all the fuel out of the fuel system and squirt 'storage seal' into the plug holes and carburettors. It looks like white shaving cream and prevents fuel and oil gelling up in the combustion chambers. It also stops condensation and rusting within the bore (bigger engines have chromed bores, and moisture will lift the chrome).

14

A quicker method is to warm up the engine and, while it is running, squirt marine two-stroke oil into the carburettor air inlets. Then remove the fuel line. While the engine is burning off the fuel in the system the whole inside of the engine oils up and will be protected. This is less effective than storage seal, but better than nothing.

Drain the fuel tanks and turn them upside down with the tops off to prevent a build-up of water and the resultant rust. It is worth noting here that the modern additives in petrol (gasoline) break down after about three months and the fuel goes stale, as well as attracting moisture. So remove any old fuel left in the outboard system and dispose of it in an environmentally-friendly way. Also consider fuel treatment additives.

Remove the battery from the boat and put it on a piece of wood. Trickle-charge it for a short while each month.

Re-commissioning outboards

At the beginning of the new season replace the battery, refuel the system and fire up the engine in a water tank or with the engine muffs connected to a hosepipe. Always turn the water on first, and never exceed 1500 rpm.

The storage seal will burn off after a few starts. Clouds of smoke will pour out and the plugs might oil up and need cleaning. Persevere. Within a short time the engine should be running smoothly.

Winterisation: inboard diesels

Manufacturers will have their own recommended programmes for engine storage, but if you have no information you should try the following.

Before removing the craft from the water:

1   Start the engine and warm it up. This makes the oil more fluid.
2   Stop the engine and drain off the engine oil.
3   Replace the sump plug and refill with recommended anti-corrosion oil to the bottom mark on the oil dipstick.

4   Mix two litres of diesel fuel with one litre of recommended anti-corrosion oil in a clean container.

5   Disconnect the fuel line and hold the end in this container. Start up the engine and run it for 10-15 minutes, then close it down.

14   With the craft out of the water, take the following steps. (Note that there are two types of cooling system: the engine may use a closed system with a heat exchanger unit like that of a car, whereas a sterndrive uses water from the sea for cooling and has its own impeller.)

1   Drain off water from the engine coolant system and replace with anti-freeze solution as recommended.

2   Mix a strong solution of correct anti-freeze with fresh water and, using a hose attached to the lower leg water intake, run up the engine at idling speed to circulate the mixture. Stop the engine and remove the impeller.

3   Unscrew each of the fuel injectors and add to each cylinder about a teaspoon of the recommended anti-corrosion oil.

4   De-gunk the engine and transmission and wash everything down with a solution of soap-based washing-up liquid (not detergent). All the dirt and waste will fall into the engine compartment.

5   Thoroughly clean the engine compartment. This is a difficult job, but one well worth doing. Use a rag, sponges, de-gunk, washing-up liquid and fresh water until it is polished and shiny. This work will pay dividends when you come to sell or exchange your boat.

6   Dry off and coat or spray with marine water displacement oil for total protection. Lubricate all the cables and linkages.

7   Remove the battery. Trickle-charge it regularly. If you disconnected the hose to the impeller pump on the sterndrive, reassemble it now.

Re-commissioning inboards

1   Put in a fully-charged battery.

2   Drain the anti-corrosion oil and replace with the recommended engine oil.

3   Re-install the water pump impeller to the stern drive.

4   Remove the fuel injectors and crank over the engine several times to remove excess oil from the cylinders. Replace the injectors.

5   Replace the fuel filter and fill the tank with fresh diesel fuel.

6   Check all lines and connections, and check that all seacocks and bungs are in position.

7   Lower the craft into the water, open the outside water valve and check all the connections for leaks. Run the engine as soon as possible. If the engine turns over but does not fire properly, there could be air in the fuel system. See the section on bleeding a diesel fuel system.

Hull maintenance: rigid hulls

Most rigid powerboat hulls are made of glass reinforced plastic (GRP, commonly known as glassfibre). This requires very little work to maintain it in good condition.

Hose down the hull with fresh water after every session, and wash down with a bio-degradable washing-up liquid in warm water at least twice a year. Use glassfibre cleaner to remove obstinate grease marks, and polish with a non-silicone polish at least once a year.

Eliminate small surface scratches with fine wet-and-dry sandpaper, a rubbing compound and polish. Deeper scores will need repairing with epoxy filler: undercut the edges and clean it out with acetone before applying the filler. Overfill slightly and allow 24 hours to cure. Then rub down as above.

Major damage is best repaired professionally in case the strength of the hull has been compromised.

14

Hull maintenance: inflatables

Hose down with fresh water each time the boat is used. Use a bio-degradable washing-up solution to remove mud, sand and general dirt. Use neat white spirit to remove oil and fuel spillage and then wash off.

Tube pressure

Keep the craft inflated at the correct pressure or fully deflated. The actual amount of air needed depends on the weather. If the craft is too highly inflated in hot weather it will literally pop unless fitted with automatic valves. Add or remove air as necessary. If you keep the hull deflated, wash and dry it and use French chalk or cheap talcum powder on the outside (only) before putting it in storage.

Repairs

Keep a puncture repair kit on board to get you home. Pinprick punctures are easily repaired using a technique familiar to every bicycle owner. The hull must be dry.

1   Clean the surface with surgical spirit. Mark the damage.
2   Roughen the surface and the inside of the repair patch with medium sandpaper. Remove dust.
3   Apply three coats of the recommended glue to each surface. Allow the first coat to dry for about 30 minutes to ensure that it soaks in. The following two coats will need about 10 minutes each to dry.
4   When dry, press the patch and rubber tube firmly together.
5   Remove air bubbles by using a pressure pad, working from the centre of the patch outwards to ensure a good seal.

The most common reasons why repairs fail are:

- the tube is wet from water
- the glue surfaces are not perfectly dry
- the patch is too small or not central
- insufficient drying time has been allowed

14

Rips and tears need to be professionally repaired. They usually have to be stitched and double-patched (a small patch fixed on, followed by a large one on top).

- Major repairs are carried out from the inside of the tube first, followed by the outside patch, more for cosmetic purposes than functional.

Valves

Standard valves can start to leak after a while. Apply a small amount of grease to the inside of each protective cap and tighten it to provide a good seal.

Trailer maintenance

Trailers require continual attention if they are to last. Follow this maintenance programme.

1   Wash down thoroughly with fresh water after recovery from the sea or river. Check the galvanised metal box tube for cracks. Check 'U' bolts and metal angle supports for failure. Remove all end caps. They trap water.

2   Grease the ball cup and locking handle regularly.

3   Strip down and grease the jockey wheel after every six launchings. This only takes a few minutes.

4   Wash down and either grease the winch handle mechanism or spray it with water-displacement oil. Check the winch cable for rust and wear; replace if necessary. Alternatively, use webbing as this is safer, but check it regularly for fraying.

5   Check the snap shackle connection to the winch cable or webbing.

6   Periodically check all nuts and bolts on the trailer and tighten if necessary.

7   Periodically check the adjustment arms and rollers for positioning. They tend to work loose and shift position. The hull could be damaged if it is incorrectly supported on its trailer

Wheels

If the trailer is left unattended for long periods, the wheels can become corroded, the bearings may seize up, the tyres will deflate and the sidewalls will crack.

Follow this maintenance programme.

1   Spray the inside and outside of the wheels and suspension units with water-displace-ment oil before storing. Avoid spilling oil on the brake shoes if the trailer is braked.

2   Keep the tyres at the correct pressure.

3   Keep bearings with external grease nipples very well greased with a recommended grease which does not react with salt water. There are spring-grease-loaded hub caps on the market which will prevent water, sand and salt creeping into the bearings.

4   Hold the top of the tyre and rock it inwards and outwards. If there is move-ment, adjust or replace the bearings. Always carry a spare set of wheel bearings. Best to carry a spare hub set.

5   Ensure the tyres meet the minimum legal requirements of the country you are in. Check for tyre tread depth, check the tyre walls for damage, cracking and splitting and check the air pressure.

6   Always carry a spare wheel and tyre.

Changing wheels
Carry a small hand hydraulic jack for lifting the trailer and boat to change a wheel. Keep the trailer attached to the vehicle and wedge the other wheel.

It is often difficult to purchase spare tyres on their own. Many dealers only sell a wheel complete with the tyre fitted, because so many wheels actually corrode away and fall off the trailer.

14

Robert Owen using a hand-held computer to diagnose faults in an inboard engine.

15 Get knotted

If pulling a boat using a warp, first go around a cleat or bollard. Pull the standing part with one hand and take up the slack with the other.

Rope work

Competence in handling ropes and knots should be second nature to boat handlers. You need ropes for mooring, anchoring and towing, as well as rescue. Rope work is no mystery; it just takes practice. Remember that a little dexterity with ropes could save your life.

Always use good quality ropes of the right material. The rope must be strong enough for the job required of it but at the same time it must fit comfortably in the hand and be pleasant to handle. The rope should be thick enough to be gripped in the hand without feeling the need to twist it around the hand. Ropes twisted around the hand or wrist can take time to be released. So please don't do it.

Types of rope

If you enter a chandlers you will be confronted by a mass of coloured ropes of all different sizes and prices. For the anchor I would suggest you look for a multiplait nylon rope. It is very flexible, doesn't kink and doesn't float. It remains manageable and easy to stow. Use a thickness of around 10–12 mm.

For mooring and general warps I suggest something similar to the 3-strand standard polyester rope, which is absolutely ideal for both purposes. If you purchase the correct rope it should be rot proof, waterproof and abrasion resistant. I work with 10 or 12mm thickness because it fits into the hand well.

The painter could be made up of something similar to a 3-strand Marstron, which is a multifilament polypropylene. This is a lightweight rope that floats and which would also be ideal for the warps, the fenders and lines. If the painter is a floating line it is easily recoverable if it goes over the side. Remember bow lines (painter) need to be less than the length of the boat.

For a lifeline or a heaving line I would suggest that you look at something similar to the 8-plait Marstron, which is again a multifilament polypropylene that is very strong, easy to handle, coils nicely and floats. It also comes in a variety of different colours.

If it is being used as a heaving line it obviously doesn't necessarily need to be 10mm in thickness. In this case I would suggest a light line with a weighted end if it's used for heaving.

If you are leaving a marina and are leaving your mooring lines behind on the pontoon, I suggest that you use 3-strand hardy hemp, which again is polypropylene and not very expensive. The mooring lines can be left in the correct length so that when you return to your pontoon all you need to do is pick them up.

If you separate the trailer from the vehicle and use rope to pull the trailer and boat up out of the water, you will need a very strong and easy-to-handle rope. It is going to receive a massive amount of abuse and therefore needs to have a breaking strain at least twice as much as the boat you are pulling up out of the water. I use 31/2 ton breaking strain. This is far greater than required but I believe it is wise to work on the side of caution.

Care of ropes

After use wash rope thoroughly with fresh water. Remove sand, grit and mud, and hang up to dry. Do not leave wet rope in the bottom of the boat. Avoid the pretty coil (cheesing), as this is difficult to use when it dries out. It is better to loop the rope along the side of the boat if you do not have the facilities to hang it up.

Types of knot

Bowline
This is probably the most useful knot of them all. It can be used for mooring, joining two ropes together, towing the boat and trailer out of the water and single-handed looping around a person in the water.

15

All the time there is a load on it a bowline cannot collapse or slip. It can always be quickly undone once the load is off, regardless of how much weight has been put on it. If the pressure will not be constant use the loose end as a half hitch around the loop to make the knot secure. There are at least three different ways of tying a bowline.

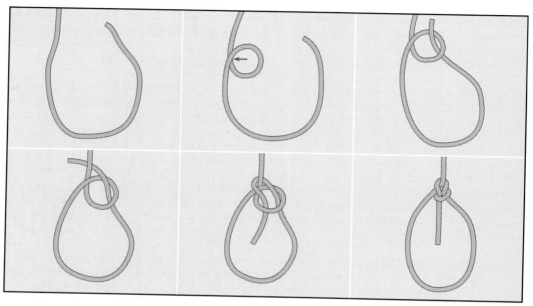

Clove hitch

This is useful for forming a strong hitch in the middle of a rope that is attached at both ends. It is the one we use on the towing ball of the vehicle for retrieving the boat and trailer. However, do not use a clove hitch if the load is very heavy as it can tighten up to such a point that you will not be able to undo it. If you are pulling a very heavy trailer out using a ball hitch and rope, loop the rope around the ball hitch many times and then ask someone to walk with the end of the rope.

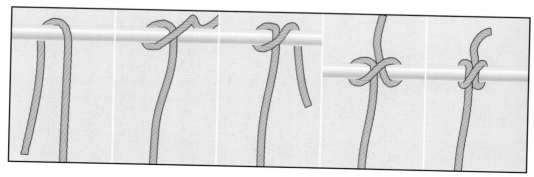

Each turn around the ball hitch is on top of each other and this will hold and pull a boat up out of the water. Once it is out all you have to do is uncoil the rope off the ball hitch. If you are making the clove hitch between the two ends, take the rope and form two loops in the same direction. Place the top loop behind the other loop and drop both over the ball hitch or bollard.

The load can be applied from both directions at the same time or from one direction only. If you are forming the clove hitch over a post then it is just a turn around the post, cross over and back through itself as shown.

15

Round turn and two half hitches
This is another very useful hitch and excellent for tying up to mooring buoys. However, if I am leaving the boat overnight I will put several more hitches in place just to be on the safe side. For the round turn, put two loops around the ring or post. Then finish off with two half hitches. They should look like a clove hitch secured around the standing part of this rope. In other words, both half hitches must be formed the same way otherwise they will work loose.

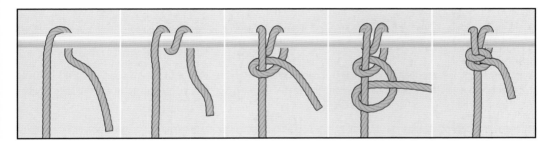

Fisherman's bend
This is a knot for more permanent use and one that often ends by being cut off. Start the round turn and two half hitches but take the end and make the first half hitch back between the turns against the post and then finish off with a half hitch. Fishermen often use this knot for tying twine to fishhooks. The benefit of this knot is that it will not come undone and will eventually become tighter and tighter. It is ideal around chain that is underwater.

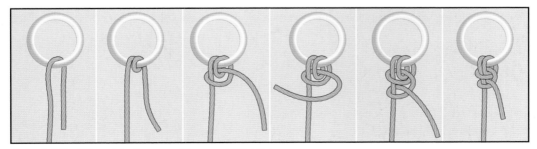

Only slightly different to the round turn and 2½ hitches.

Sheet bend

This is used for joining two ropes together and is especially valuable if they are of different thickness. Both loose ends can be seized (whipped with twine) to the standing part to make a more permanent bend. Two circuits round and you have a double sheet bend. The double sheet bend is more secure.

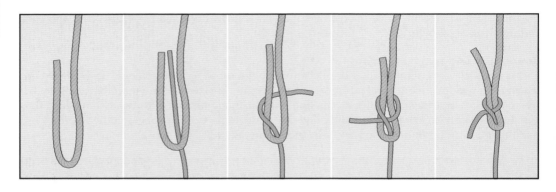

Rolling hitch

A rolling hitch is excellent for a side pull on another rope or wire but make sure the pull is from the direction shown. If you wish to pull from the other direction you have to start the hitch from the other direction.

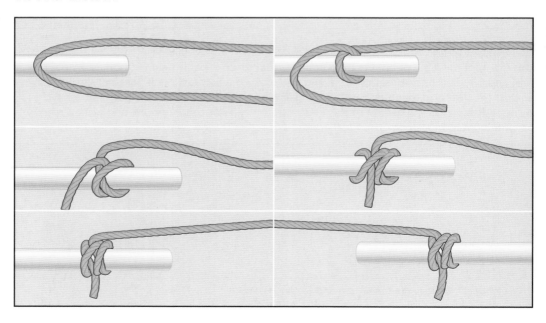

The classic figure of eight with lock off.

Camel hitch
The camel hitch will take the strain from both directions and can easily be undone even if soaking wet. It is excellent for towing a line of dinghies astern on a towline, especially where young people may well get the rolling hitch the wrong way around.

Heaving lines
It is well worth having a heaving line on board your boat. This is the floating line coiled in such a way that if the coils are separated one half of the line can be thrown and the other half of the line follows on.

Also consider carrying a throw bag on board. This is a bag already packed with line and ready to be thrown.

A correctly coiled rope will fall out of the hand when thrown.

Working on the deck, it is easy to lasso the cleat or bollard.

16 Rule of the road

The IRPCS (International Regulations for Preventing Collisions at Sea) are the rules for preventing collisions at sea. They apply to all waters that are navigable by seagoing vessels. Most estuaries lead eventually to narrow rivers. Access is often through locks and/or by waiting for high tide to give sufficient lift of water to allow movement of larger boats. It therefore follows that the rules are also used for inland water.

Where the area of inland water is large, as in Lake Windermere, the rules have been adapted and local regulations have been added to cover the specific needs of the lake and its environment.

This table lists the rules in chronological order. The third column contains my interpretation of the rules as they pertain to sportsboats

Rule 1 Application	This applies to all vessels on the high seas and all waters connected with the seas that are navigable by seagoing vessels. This does not include inland locked water.	Local regulations may include all the IRPCS and may be applied to inland water.
Rule 2 Responsibility	Rules shall not override commonsense. Remember the expression, 'Rules are made for the guidance of wise men and the obedience of fools'. Responsibility rests with the skipper at all times and in order to be safe he may depart from the rules.	Never assume you have right of way over another vessel even if you are on its starboard side. Always wait for the vessel to first give way.
Rule 3 Definitions	Underway – not attached to the ground. Making way – moving through the water. Power-driven vessel – anything using power.	May not be moving through the water. The importance here is the shapes and lights displayed. A sailing vessel with sails up and using power is a powered vessel within the rules.
Rule 4 Application	This states that the rules apply in any condition of visibility.	

Rule 5 Lookout	Should be kept by sight and hearing and all other available means.	The difficulty with regard to a sportsboat is the speed and the side-on approach of other high-speed vessels. Be aware of blind areas and spray in the eyes.
Rule 6 Safe speed	A speed sufficiently slow to enable you to take avoidance action in good time to prevent collision. Yachts and larger vessels might be on autopilot; it takes time to respond. Crew might be seasick! Large vessels may be restricted in their ability to manoeuvre. Comply with speed limits.	Other craft may be less manoeuvrable. Slow down and LOOK before turning – never assume the water is clear! Slow at night or in restricted visibility.
Rule 7 Risk of collision Bearing remains constant: risk of collision	States that a skipper must use all available means to determine whether a risk of collision exists. For the small-boat skipper this invariably means checking that the approaching ship remains on a steady course (bearing). If the angle between the ships remains steady the two will collide.	One must have sufficient room to manoeuvre prior to an alteration of course.
Rule 8 Action to avoid collision	It requires a manoeuvre to be taken early and boldly. An alteration of course must be immediately obvious to the other vessel. An alteration to starboard (right) will extricate one from most situations.	Never turn to port (left) for a boat on your port side. Never alter course into the path of another. Never try to pass ahead of another craft. A sportsboat following another must be aware that the craft in front may turn in any direction and may even carry out a 180° alteration of course.

16

Rule 9 Narrow channels	SEA and RIVERS Keep to starboard side (right). Never impede larger vessels. Cross channels with care.	Sportsboats should keep outside deep-water channels and remain over the shallow areas away from larger craft.
Rule 10 Traffic Separation Schemes 	In operation where the passing of large ships requires precise routes to avoid a collision – congested water.	Small craft should, if possible, use Inshore Traffic Zones. If small craft have to use a traffic lane they must follow the correct direction for the lane and not impede larger vessels. If it is necessary to cross a traffic lane, make sure your heading is at right angles to the lane, cross as rapidly as possible and keep clear of vessels that are using the lane.
Rule 11 Lights	Should carry lights prescribed in the full rules.	See Almanac.
Rule 12 Sailing vessels	Avoid and/or give way to all sailing vessels.	
Rule 13 Overtaking vessels a) Overtaking: keeps clear until clear ahead b) Vessel being overtaken maintains course and speed c) Angle for overtaking boat anywhere within (white sternlight arc) 135° d) Don't turn the overtaking into a crossing situation i.e. boat being overtaken looks before they turn	The overtaking vessel keeps clear until clear ahead.	

16

Rule 14	Alter course to starboard (see	
Head on situation	sketches).	
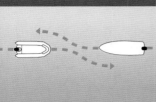		
Rule 15 **Crossing**	The vessel with the other on her starboard side shall keep clear. The starboard side is the GREEN-GIVE-WAY-SECTOR The Rules say you 'should avoid crossing ahead'. It is also dangerous seamanship to cross the bows of another vessel at close quarters.	Referred to as the YIELD ZONE on US boats. Slow down and allow the other vessel to pass ahead and/or alter course to starboard (see sketches).
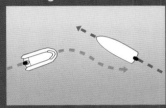		
Rule 16 **Action by the 'give-way vessel'**	The give-way vessel must take early action to keep clear.	
Rule 17 **Action by the 'stand-on vessel'**	The stand-on vessel must hold its speed and course. If it becomes quickly apparent that the other vessel is not going to give way, the stand-on vessel may take whatever action is necessary to avoid a collision.	If the stand-on vessel starts to deviate, chaos will quickly follow due to confusion over who needs to keep clear. It may be prudent to take action to starboard – 180° and show your stern.
 As A, you should normally maintain your course. But if B takes no action, stop or turn right NOT left.		

16

Rule 18 Responsibility between vessels	The more manoeuvrable vessel shall keep clear of the less manoeuvrable vessel.	A vessel under power gives way to a vessel:
		▪ Not under command (NUC);
		▪ Restricted in the ability to manoeuvre (RAM);
		▪ Engaged in fishing;
		▪ A sailing vessel (unless it's motoring).

If you are thinking about moving about at night first study the lights on buoys found on the chart. Then make a study of the navigation lights found on a variety of boats.

All the above IRPCS are applicable in the dark.

Lights and shapes

The lights shown by various vessels fit into two categories:

Navigation lights.
These are the lights that any vessel must show from sunset to sunrise and also in restricted visibility. They vary according to a vessel's size and there are different lights for vessels under power and under sail.

Distinguishing lights (and shapes).
In addition to showing navigation lights, vessels employed in certain activities (eg towing or fishing) or in certain situations (eg not under command) also show distinguishing lights by night and shapes by day. For this reason it is logical to list shapes and distinguishing lights together.

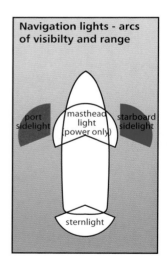

Navigation lights - arcs of visibilty and range

Power-driven vessels underway (RULE 23)

Stern	Port side	Bow

Under 7 m and speed under 7 knots

May show all-round white light only.

Under 12 m

May show all-round white light (instead of masthead light and sternlight) + sidelights.

under 50 m

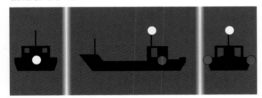

Masthead light - sidelights and sternlight.

over 50 m

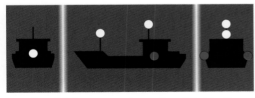

Masthead light - second masthead light aft and higher - sidelights - sternlight.

Vessels under Sail (Rule 25)

Stern	Port side	Bow

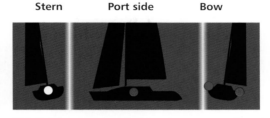

Sidelights and sternlight only - no masthead light.

But small yachts (under 20 m) may combine all these into one tricolour at the masthead.

A sailing yacht when motor sailing shows the same lights as a power vessel. So engine on, steaming light on.

By day: Sailing vessels using their engines for propulsion but with sails hoisted should show a cone, point down, forward.

Vessels at anchor (RULE 30)

Under 50 m
All round white
light forward.

A second white
light aft (lower
than forward light).

Towing (Rule 24)

The tow is measured from the stern of the tug to the stern of the tow.

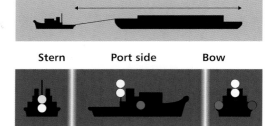

Stern   Port side   Bow

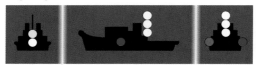

Tug's lights when tow is less than 200 m.

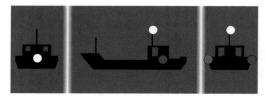

Tug's lights when tow is more that 200 m.

If the tug is more than 50 m it will also carry a second (white) masthead light aft of, and higher than, the forward one.

Vessel being towed.

By day: Diamonds, only needed if tow exceeds 200 m.

Diving tender

Flag 'A' or rigid replica.

Although diving tenders rarely operate at night, when doing so they must show the vertical red/white/red lights indicating restricted ability to manoeuvre.

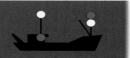

Vessels Trawling (Rule 26)

A vessel trawling (ie towing some kind of net) shows all-round green-over-white lights. Show regular navigation lights when making way, but not when stopped.

Vessel fishing (Rule 26)

All-round red-over-white lights, plus sidelights and sternlight (if making way).

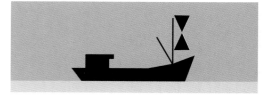

By day: Trawlers and fishing vessels show a shape consisting of two cones with their points together.

16

Holding ground

Check that the sea, lake or riverbed is good holding ground. Ask someone who has local knowledge, and check on the chart for the designated anchorages. The chart will also indicate areas where anchoring is prohibited. Amongst the obvious prohibited areas are those where electric power lines run, deep-water navigational channels, warship exercise areas, among moorings and between ferry terminals. Do not anchor too close to other vessels: remember that they, and you, could swing with the wind and tide and may collide.

On a point of etiquette, the first person to the anchorage and anchored has priority. The second person coming in avoids the first, the third person coming in avoids the first and second and so on. Where sportsboats are without depth sounders, one will have to check the chart and tide tables to find the depth of water under the keel.

17

Anchoring technique

1   Check the area and decide which is the stronger force – tide or wind? If you are unsure, come into neutral and check your drift against stationary objects such as other anchored craft, trees on the shore and buildings. (Use transits.)

2   Having found the place where you wish to come to rest, engage forward gear and slowly drive to a position ahead of where you wish to stop, pointing into the wind and/or tide. As you start to drift backwards, instruct the crew to lower the anchor over the bow. If you are anchoring from a small boat this will be done from the side of the boat. It is, therefore, important that you turn the helm slightly away from the wind or current so that the boat drifts back away from the anchor, rather than over it.

Releasing the anchor

3   When the anchor and chain touch the bottom, the weight goes off the warp. Read off the bands on the warp (or estimate) and multiply by five or six. Slowly let out this length of warp as the boat drifts backwards and sideways. Do not expect the anchor to hold until the line is out to the required depth. Therefore do not attach the rope (or make secure) to the boat until the correct depth is out.

4   When you are satisfied that sufficient warp is out, nudge astern. This takes out the slack in the warp. There is only one place for the warp to be tied to and that is at the bow. However, if you are in a small sportsboat you do not want to balance on the bow. Instead take the painter back to the cockpit and, using a sheet bend onto the anchor warp, tie it off and allow the boat to settle back pulling on the painter. When the boat settles down the anchor warp is attached

17

Wait until the boat starts to drift astern or sideways, then lower the anchor.

to the painter, the painter is attached to the front of the boat and the boat sets at the correct angle to the wind and current. Once the line is attached to the painter or it is pulling from the front of the boat engage reverse and go astern slowly to dig the anchor in. The boat will lurch gently to a stop once the anchor gains a hold.

5   If the anchor does not hold, the boat will keep drifting, and here you have two choices: To go into neutral, motor forward retrieving the warp, untie the painter and let out more warp before attempting to tie off. Or raise the anchor completely and try again.

6   As soon as the anchor holds firm, go into neutral. If you attach the warp to the side of the boat, the boat will come to rest at about 45° to the wind and/or tide. This position is dangerous because you are offering the side of the boat to the wind and current. In strong winds the warp going over the side of the boat will drag the side down into the waves and you stand a very serious risk of swamping.

7   Avoid anchoring from the stern because in a strong current or wind it will pull the boat under water.

Small boats are ideal for beach landing.

With an offshore wind take the anchor ashore and bed it in.

Tidal waters

At sea, or in a tidal river, you will need to pay or lay out more warp to allow for rising tides. As the tide falls the boat will drift back further and swing round in the tidal stream. Make sure you have room to swing.

Transits

When you are satisfied that the anchor is holding, check for any fixed objects in the vicinity that can line up to form transits (see page 0). Transit alignments define your position. Recheck from time to time to make sure the anchor is not dragging – but remember to allow for tide and wind effects. If you cannot see any good alignments take compass bearings on isolated objects such as buoys and towers and recheck these at intervals.

17

Raising the anchor

Do a propeller check, then start up the engine and warm up.

The crew of a small sportsboat can slowly pull in the warp and the boat will creep forward through the water without using the engine. Heavier craft will probably need a push with the engine but be careful not to overrun the anchor warp. I suggest powering gently towards the anchor.

As the boat moves forward the crew gathers up the anchor warp and puts it into the anchor box or anchor locker. The crew continually advises the helm as to the position of the warp. For the moment ignore the painter; that can be detached later. If the anchor warp is flaked down into the box it is ready for the next time.

Once the anchor has been recovered, push the boat out into the deeper water and start the engine.

Make sure all equipment is onboard before moving away.

17

When the boat is directly over the anchor the warp will be vertical, and a good heave should break the anchor out of the seabed.

The boat is now drifting, but do not engage gear until the anchor is clear of the water. Keep the anchor and chain clear from the side of the boat to prevent damage. Remove any mud and place the chain and then the anchor on top of the warp in the box. Check the direction of drift, and decide whether to move ahead or astern and slowly drive away.

Tripping lines

What should you do if the anchor refuses to come up? The conventional type of tripping line used on large boats creates too much confusion of rope for a small powerboat, but you can rig an automatic tripping device. If you are anchoring on an unknown seabed, it might prove useful.

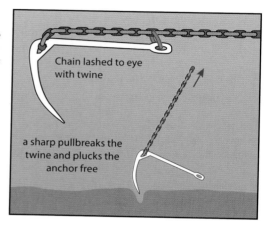

Chain lashed to eye with twine

a sharp pullbreaks the twine and plucks the anchor free

Set the anchor up with the chain attached (shackled) to the hook end. Attach the chain to the eye in the shaft with thin twine as shown in the diagram. If the anchor fails to lift, a good sharp tug on the warp will break the twine and the anchor should lift free from the shackled end. Continually check the condition of the twine otherwise the anchor could trip out of the seabed under normal use. The twine will perish and could need replacing regularly. Note that this method is not suitable for a heavy boat, which will simply snap the twine as soon as the anchor bites in the seabed.

Anchor stuck with no tripping line

If the anchor refuses to come up and you have not set a tripping line there are one or two things that could be tried.

You have moved your boat above the anchor and found that it will not lift. First try to reverse in the opposite direction to which you set the anchor. With luck this will break it out. You should have attached the painter to the anchor line so that the pull comes from the most secure part of the boat just under the bow. Larger sportsboats will use the cleat on the deck and the rope will be over the bow roller. It is worth trying this manoeuvre a few times.

If this fails I would suggest that you then tie a fender to the anchor warp and cast it off. Enlist the help of a larger boat to try and lift the anchor.

Emergency anchoring

It is quite possible that a problem may occur when you are out on the water that leads to a breakdown and you find that you are without power. The problem could be damage, mechanical, electrical or a rope around the propeller. Assess the situation. Where are you in relation to other boats and to deep water? How far can you afford to drift before you need to consider anchoring? Consider the depth of water. It is a pointless exercise with 45m (150ft) of line and anchor to try and anchor in 45m (150ft) of water. If possible, allow the boat to drift out of any main navigation channel and into a shallow area, then lower the anchor. This will prevent you from going onto a lee shore. It will also leave you secure in the water, enabling you to organise repair or recovery by tow.

17

Special circumstances

If the wind is blowing onto the shore (lee shore), bring the boat up and around into wind and waves. Set the anchor far enough off the beach for it to hold in deep water. Check that the anchor is holding. Once it is holding you are in a position to switch off the engine and raise the leg of the outboard engine.

Pay out more and more line until the boat comes into a shallow area. The bow will be facing the breaking waves. When close, make the line secure and the crew can go over the stern into shallow water taking another line or secondary anchor ashore and again making this secure. This is an ideal method for working off a sheltered sandy beach where you could then move the picnic and barbecue ashore for a party. If the water is deep, then this line from the stern of the boat to the shore becomes a 'lifeline'. All crew going ashore can swim along this line, returning to the boat along the same route. The last person unties the line and holds on as the crew onboard drags them back to the boat. I often use this method when anchored off deserted islands in the Caribbean.

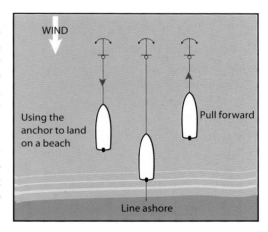

Using the anchor to land on a beach

WIND

Pull forward

Line ashore

This method can also be used successfully for a rescue of a boat actually on a lee shore.

18 Towing

If you break down, check your location. If there is any chance that you are going to drift into danger, consider anchoring immediately. Then decide if you have the ability to rectify the problem.

Preliminary considerations

- Where are you?
- What is the risk?
- What is your destination - lee shore?
- Why have you broken down?

If you cannot restart the engine or rectify the fault you may be there for a long time. Meanwhile the boat will swing sideways and roll with the waves in a most uncomfortable fashion, and you need to do something to steady it up.

Side tow: Small vessel pulling larger boat.

Anchor or sea anchor?

Anchoring is best because the bow will be brought around to face the tide/wind, but if this is not possible you may have to stream a drogue from the bow. (A parachute drogue is referred to as a sea anchor.)

How to obtain a tow

Consider methods of attracting attention and if these fail resort to the radio. As soon as the rescue craft comes alongside discuss your requirements and if a tow is possible ask how much it is going to cost you. The RNLI do not charge for their service but sensible donations are appreciated.

Agreement

Establishing a financial agreement is vital. It may be 'It's OK mate, it might be me next time' or, 'I want twenty quid an hour, OK?' This is a contract and binding in law.

If you are doing the towing remember the job must be within your capabilities. If you damage the craft you are towing, you could end up footing the bill!

Setting up the tow - long tow

Whatever you agree you must ensure that the line used for towing is your line and fixed to your boat. A good strong point is under the bow at the D or U bolt, so use your painter attached to a 20 metre line. It's for you to pass this line to the boat that is prepared to do the tow. Your line needs to be made secure at the stern of the towing boat. It is usually useful for them to set up a bridle so the pull is directly amidships (in the middle) behind the engine.

Discuss speed of tow. You will probably need to move your weight to the stern to allow the bow to rise and follow in a relatively straight line. (If the bow is down it can veer from side to side inducing a capsize.) The length of tow must be long enough for your boat not to ram the back of the boat in front when moving down the waves. Request that they motor off gently to take up the slack and to tow your boat home at displacement speed. If you are travelling into the waves all will be well, but if the waves are overtaking you they will tend to push your boat forwards, putting slack into the tow rope which may foul the towing boat's propeller. Prevent this by pulling a makeshift sea anchor astern, such as a loop of rope or a bucket. This will slow you down and keep the tow rope taut. Once into a harbour it may pay to change the long tow into a side tow.

Side tow

Request the towing boat to come alongside you (with fenders) and ask them to position their stern a short distance behind the stern of your boat. Take the painter from the towing boat and attach this to a strong point at the stern of your craft. Make sure it is secure, because this is the rope that will take most of the strain. Use a round turn and two half hitches so you can release the line even if it is under load. Use two smaller lines to keep the bow and stern of each boat together - these are breast ropes. For any manoeuvring astern you will require another line from the stern of the towing boat to the front of your boat. In other words, bow spring, stern spring, two breast ropes. The reason the stern of the towing boat is behind your disabled craft is for them to have manoeuvrability.

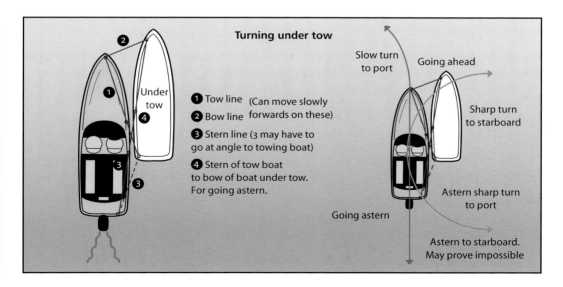

Turning under tow

Under tow

❶ Tow line (Can move slowly forwards on these)
❷ Bow line
❸ Stern line (3 may have to go at angle to towing boat)
❹ Stern of tow boat to bow of boat under tow. For going astern.

Slow turn to port

Going ahead

Sharp turn to starboard

Going astern

Astern sharp turn to port

Astern to starboard. May prove impossible

18

If you have rafted up the towing boat on your starboard side the turns to port will be very tight, whereas the turns to starboard will be very slow and difficult. It's like having a very wide twin-engined boat with only one engine working.

Two boats alongside in this fashion can be brought together onto their respective trailers for recovery.

Salvage

Through no personal fault or error, you may need outside assistance. It could be a serious rescue or just a simple pull or shove in the right direction. Mention the words cost, contract, salvage and invariably the yachtsman will say, 'it's ok as long as we use our own rope for making up the tow'. Oh, if only life was that simple!

Easy and quick way to join two ropes. Bowline cannot be undone under load but round turn and two half hitches can.

To warrant salvage a danger must have existed. Some dangers can be easily identified, such as a vessel drifting onto a lee shore and onto the rocks, with the anchor deployed and found not to be holding. A vessel coming to assist would need to calculate its own risk to its crew and to its own potential loss on the same lee shore. The effort of rescue in this case would be as high as the risk.

It may even be possible to claim salvage by standing by and offering advice or by making equipment available such as pumps, ropes, fenders, fire extinguishers or more commonly by passing a towing warp to the boat in danger.

The salvers could make a claim against a boat in danger if they could prove that the crew lacked skill or knowledge. A crew that has just popped out to sea for five minutes without any basic equipment puts them-selves and the rescuers at risk. A further claim could be made if the condition of the vessel was such that it became a liability to the crew on board.

Tow of convenience

The normal yacht insurance policy covers salvage but does not cover a tow of convenience e.g. where you are becalmed and late for dinner. The boat has to be in real danger and life at risk.

It is therefore vital with a tow of convenience that the crew of the towed vessel establishes how much the tow is going to cost. Most yachtsmen agree a tow out of courtesy to each other. This is not the same if you use the services of commercial craft - they will normally expect to be paid an hourly fee or a 'one off' charge for the tow. You are unlikely to reclaim the cost of this from your insurance company.

Lloyds Open Agreement

If however the vessel is in danger and life at risk the situation may dictate that the recovery will be under the term of salvage. I suggest you resort to the Lloyds Form of Salvage Agreement, which was first introduced in 1890 and works on a 'no cure no pay' basis.

This is a simple form of salvage agreement where either:

a.   The sum or fee to be paid shall be decided out on the water or

b.   The whole business of finance is turned over to your insurance company for them to negotiate directly with the salver. No fee is mentioned and Lloyds become the arbitrators.

18

In all cases the full facts will need to be recorded including time, day, date and place including the risk to the vessel being rescued and also the salver. It is important to support this information with the Ship's Log, a chart covering the area showing the history prior to the incident and relevant information on the weather conditions, the forecast and also tidal information if applicable. Similar information will be required for any other form of insurance claim.

If a salvage claim goes to court the court will examine the value of the vessels concerned, the facts of the case and also the degree of skill shown in the salvage.

Notes It is also important that you should not disclose the value of the boat to the claimant.

Remember also that you can be liable for any damage that you cause to the vessel that you are towing, if it can be proved that you were negligent. Never take onboard a tow or try a recovery that is too large for your boat to be able to handle. A contract works both ways.

There is also a responsibility attached to the crew on board the boat being salved, that they should make every effort to ensure that their vessel is handled in a seamanlike manner and to that end assist the salver in his rescue attempt.

Tow ropes

Question - so why do we need to use our own towrope?

Answer - A claim could be made by a vessel, standing by in an emergency, that she assisted the vessel that required a tow by supplying her own towrope. If possible try to set up your own tow. Unless you are genuinely in danger never accept assistance from another vessel without first making it absolutely clear that you have the situation in hand and that the tow, if accepted, is a helpful aid to saving time.

Mishaps can happen to anyone, but good training, sound seamanship and a well-found craft go a long way to eliminate all but the most unexpected occurrence.

19 Waterskiing

There must always be two in the boat: helm to drive, crew to observe.

This book is about using boats so we are not going to tell you here how to waterski, for there are plenty of other books available that do this, but we will tell you a little about the sport and the equipment you should use.

Family sport

First and foremost waterskiing is a family sport that is enjoyed by literally all ages. There are 100-year-old skiers and, at the other extreme, one-year-old infants have been towed at slow speeds, although we would recommend starting at seven years as this is when children start to coordinate brain and muscle successfully. Because waterskiing can be taught easily, many people with disabilities also enjoy the excitement of speed over the water. To get the best results from family-type skiing you do need to use the right type of boat,

Which boat?

People have skied behind practically anything that can exceed 12mph (20kph) and that includes galloping horses, sailing catamarans, aircraft, cars, naval destroyers, helicopters, war canoes and dragon boats. However, all these feats have been by experienced skiers and are somewhat of a novelty. When choosing a boat it will help if you know whether it will mostly be used on coastal or inland waters.

Coastal

For practical and affordable family skiing on coastal waters the outboard-powered sportsboat wins hands down every time. For a boat to have the ability to turn in a reasonable length, get on the plane quickly, carry a few skis and skiers, launch without too much trouble and cope with occasional choppy water it should be between 14ft and 21ft (4.3m and 6.4m) with suitable power, which would be between 50 and 300hp depending on boat size and weight.

The most suitable engines are outboard although many prefer inboard/outdrive engines that have marinised car engines and outboard-type drives to the propeller. For both these types of engine the propeller can be tilted up to the level of the bottom of the boat, which helps in the depth of water needed for launching and recovery. Outboard engines usually have a better power to weight ratio, which again helps with usage from trailers, while inboard/outboard engines may have a slightly better fuel consumption, which these days is very significant. Maximum speed is not usually a factor because recreational skiers do not need to be towed over 36mph (58kph) and mostly they are happy with 25mph (40kph). However, acceleration is important to get novice skiers up onto the plane quickly. The choice of the right pitch prop will help.

Adjusting your engine

Most sportsboats are sold with engines and propellers that will give the best maximum speed. However, waterskiing requires very good low-speed acceleration and not necessarily maximum speed. To improve acceleration for a waterskier, fit a lower pitch propeller. All inboard/outboard engines have a range of propeller pitches and you should consult the boat manufacturer for the best advice. Choosing a lower propeller pitch is very similar to using a lower gear on a car. Usually a pitch 2–4in (5–10cm) lower than the recommended standard propeller pitch will be better for waterskiing. Be careful, however, because a lower pitch may allow you to over rev the engine at full throttle. You may wish to put a note on the instrument panel to yourself or other drivers indicating that a low pitch prop is fitted. Buying another propeller, of course, means that you always have a spare in case of damage.

Typical outboard waterski boat

(Note that the observer's seat needs to be turned around.)

In this book you will see Peter White training with an RIB, which is also what most RYA training centres use. They are possibly the most popular type of small boat sold today. RIBs have a lot of very good qualities, such as ease of launching, good

An ideal set-up for waterskiing, showing all correct equipment.

handling in rough water and gentle contact when coming alongside expensive yachts, but they are not the best for waterskiing. To enjoy family skiing you don't want to drag tired children or older relatives ignominiously over the sides of great sausage-shape tubes when they are tired at the end of skiing sessions. The techniques required are the same as those described for recovering a 'man overboard' (see chapter 10) and are not ideal for routine skiing. You should provide a proper boarding platform or boarding ladder, which is easy to do on a sportsboat-type hull. A competent observer is essential for any waterskiing. And you need them alongside you and facing the skier, not with their back to you riding a bucking bronco saddle, as in many RIBs, and shouting backwards about the skier's requests or any disasters.

Other types of boats sometimes pressed into service for waterskiing include Dell Quay Dories or Boston Whalers, which all have cathedral-shape hulls. These are great boats for yacht tenders when you don't want them to tip over as you transfer people, booze and rations, but they are not the best boats for waterskiing.

Most boats used for waterskiing on coastal water can be used on inland lakes and rivers, but the reverse is not true because many specialist ski boats designed for relatively calm water do not take well to rough seas.

Inland

If you are one of the fortunate few with access to a small lake then you have the happy option of buying a boat that is designed simply for waterskiing and with no compromises. These are generically called tournament boats but they are also the best for teaching and recreational skiing. Several manufacturers produce ranges of similar boats, which typically are about 19ft (5.8m) long. They have marinised automotive V8 engines of around 300hp and have very flat bottoms. In fact they are quite unsuitable for even mildly rough seas. The bottom surfaces include thee mid-hull fins and are designed to give the optimum wake shape for waterskiers and to continue going in a straight line when a skier may be pulling extremely hard to one side. Being built for waterskiing, the observer's seat permanently faces the skier. The pylons for the ski rope are in the centre of the boat to give best pull.

Tournament boats weigh over 2,200lb (1,000kg) so towing and launching them requires a seriously strong four-wheel drive vehicle and a good slipway. Pushing them down a beach is not an option.

The professional boat is designed to cut through the water leaving a wake perfect for waterskiing. The hull is flat, designed for flat water

Compared to the abuse that many recreational powerboats take, these boats tend to be well looked after and second-hand tournament boats can be good value for the private owner.

Many of these boats are fitted with Liquid Petroleum Gas (LPG) conversions. Fuel costs about one-third less than than for petrol-powered engines, the fuel and exhaust emissions are more eco-friendly, the bulk storage in tanks is simpler and cheaper and the engine oil is less polluted by carbon. LPG has been used for over 30 years, particularly on tournament boats operated by professional ski schools.

19

Wakeboarding boats

Many people just want to wakeboard and there are specialist boats for this sport that have been derived from tournament boats. They tend to be larger and more expensive but they produce the big wakes that wakeboarders like and, of course, they have huge towers to keep the rope high and let the wakeboarder achieve 'big air' for those aerial tricks that everyone aspires to.

Equipping a ski boat

When you have bought your ski boat, assuming it is not a tournament boat, you need to equip

The ideal wake for waterskiing

it. Quite probably the passenger seat will be facing forward, so you must turn it around to face the skier. Usually, this a simple matter but even if it gives problems you must turn it round. Next, if the boat does not have a fitted boarding platform, you must provide at least a boarding ladder to enable the skier to get back in the boat. A towing pylon is a good investment and will keep the ski rope clear of the engine and above the boat wash. Fit as large a mirror as you can. If the boat has not got a speedometer you need to fit one so that you can keep a constant speed for the skier. The best ski boats do not have obtrusive chrome cleats or handles on the deck because they catch people, wetsuits and ropes, so if your boat comes with them, consider removing surplus hardware.

Skier's equipment

All skiers must weigh a buoyancy aid designed for waterskiing. These provide valuable protection to the body's internal organs if you have a hard fall and, at the same time, allow unrestricted arm movement. You should understand that they are not the same as approved lifejackets whose big collars will float an unconscious person face up. A skier who is knocked unconscious wearing a skier's jacket (buoyancy aid) may well end up floating face down, but a ski boat will always be able to return to the skier within 20 seconds or so.

19

Why an observer is necessary

The driver must always look out for hazards ahead when towing a waterskier. On public and coastal waters these hazards may be difficult to spot, especially if the water is slightly rough. They may include swimmers, floating debris, dropped waterskis and ropes – all of which ski boats have run over on numerous occasions in the past. The observer is there not only to tell you if the skier falls but also to convey their signals about speed or wanting to end the skiing session.

The observer's position that far forward not only provides ideal observation of the waterskier, but close proximity allows for clear communication with the helm.

These are fairly obvious reasons but never forget that if your skier has an accident you will need at least two people in the boat to give effective assistance. Waterskiing is a safe sport but, as with any activity associated with speed, injuries do occur from time to time. You might need two people to get an injured skier back into the boat or you might need the observer to get in the water and stay with injured skier while you go for help.

Where to waterski

Inland water where you can launch your own boat and then waterski are very limited and often restricted to members of a club. British Water Ski has more than 140 affiliated clubs and there is an approved club within 50 miles (80km) of anywhere in England. Visit www.britishwaterski.org. uk to find details of all their affiliated centres.

Coastal waterskiing offers many opportunities, but the majority of public waters also have controlling authorities that specify where and when you can waterski. It is the driver's responsibility to find the controlling authority and clarify exactly where it is permitted to waterski.

Driving qualifications and training

The best way to learn how to a drive a waterski boat is to enrol for a course leading to the British Water Ski's Ski Boat Driving Award. More information can be obtained from www.britishwaterski.org.uk

Driving position and hands

The correct way to drive a ski boat is firstly to always be properly seated. If you are perched on the back of the seat you are not properly in control and can quite easily be thrown out. If you have a problem seeing over the bow of the boat, sit on a cushion or, if nothing else is available, your spare lifejackets. Whenever you use any powerboat on coastal waters the driver must, of course, always be attached to a kill switch. Your left hand should be on the steering wheel and the right hand on the throttle handle so that you can always adjust speed and throttle back immediately if the skier falls. Your boat is not fit for waterskiing if the steering requires two hands to turn it. After a few years' use steering systems often become stiff to operate because of corrosion and wear. The usual and most satisfactory solution is to replace the steering cable, which should be considered a routinely replaceable item and not something that lasts forever.

19

Ski patterns and returning to a fallen skier

Always drive in straight lines with a 'P' or dumb-bell-type turn at the end so that your return run is back down the centre of your own wash. This gives the skier the flattest possible water and the opportunity to improve their skiing skills with a constant boat position. Returning to a fallen skier is similar to the technique described in Man Overboard in chapter 10. You must always approach the skier on the driver's side so that they are visible at all times and always at a slow idle speed. If the skier is to come back aboard you must always switch off the engine. If the skier is going to carry on skiing and you are in crowded waters it is safer to pull the towrope

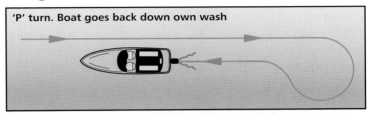

'P' turn. Boat goes back down own wash

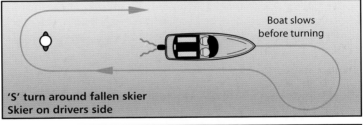

Boat slows before turning

'S' turn around fallen skier
Skier on drivers side

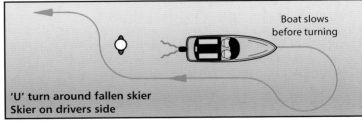

Boat slows before turning

'U' turn around fallen skier
Skier on drivers side

back into the boat after the skier falls and then throw the handle to the skier when you return to them. The danger is that other boats will run over a trailing ski rope that they cannot see. If there are no other boats about the rope can be towed at idle speed past the skier in either a 'U' or an 'S' pattern.

In either case it is essential that the skier lets the rope slide through their hands in front of their face – never behind their neck. The most dangerous equipment in waterskiing is the ski rope, whether being handled in the boat or by the skier.

19

Skier's signals

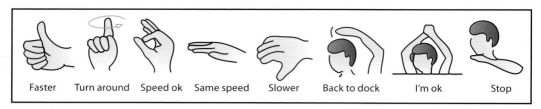

| Faster | Turn around | Speed ok | Same speed | Slower | Back to dock | I'm ok | Stop |

Communication

British Water Ski, the Maritime and Coastguard Agency, and the RNLI all recommend that waterski boats used on coastal water carry a marine band transmitter/receiver radio. They can be relatively cheap hand-held units but they are invaluable. Almost everyone uses mobile telephones and emergency operation services will always do their best to help if you have a problem but it can take a long time before you are eventually connected to the right Coastguard near the water you are on. Listening to the emergency channel 16 you may be able to direct inshore lifeboats and helicopters to your position or, because you in a fast boat, you may be able to assist other water users, such as windsurfers and sailors, who are in difficulty.

Inflatables

After buying a ski boat the first thing that many new owners acquire is some sort of inflatable water tube. However, these are definitely dangerous when used irresponsibly. When the boat does a tight turn the inflatable slides out on the whip and the riders have no control over what happens. If this slide out on the whip is near any obstruction, such as the shore, a jetty or another boat and a collision occurs, the rider may be very seriously injured or even killed. You must obey the inflatable manufacturer's recommendations for maximum speed, which in many cases is 15mph (24kph).

For coastal waterskiing: essential to carry marine radio and be qualified in its use.

Some accidents have occurred at higher speeds when the inflatable nosedives into the water like a submarine. Whenever an inflatable has more than one person aboard, helmets must be worn. The hazard is that when getting thrown about the riders may bang their heads together and receive injury. If all this sounds a bit scaremongering, it is because inflatables have many accidents with inexperienced drivers. Inflatables can be good fun for everyone, as no skills are necessary to ride them, but only if they are driven cautiously.

Family fun

Everyone in a family can be taught to waterski and it is a sport that will increase a person's self-confidence enormously. Just skiing behind a boat on one or two skis is not the end but just the beginning of all sorts of challenging things you can master. In competitive tournament skiing skills are tested with the three classic events of slalom skiing through accurately measured courses, trick skiing and jumping. Ski racing with mass starts of up to 40 boats usually takes place on coastal courses. Barefoot skiing is a long established tournament sport. Kneeboarding is both a recreational and a tournament sport. And of course the big event that most youngsters want to be part of is wakeboarding

19

And finally

When you and your friends have all learnt to ski, here is a little party trick to keep some enthusiasm in your skiing. Building a three-person pyramid looks spectacular but is really very easy. The only equipment you need is a boat powerful enough to pull three of you up on pairs of skis. Use three standard 75ft (23m) long ski ropes but it is absolutely essential that the rope and handle of the climbing person is extended to be 18in (45cm) longer than the other two ropes.

The easiest combination is two good strong skiers on the base and a very light and nimble climber. Often the best person for this is a boy or girl of about 12 whose weight is minimal for the base carriers.

First practise by tying the ropes and stretching them out on grass and then, with a catcher for the climber, let them try clambering up. The two base carriers should squat a little so that the climber can stand on their thighs before putting an arm around the carriers' necks and heaving themselves up onto their shoulders. Once the climber is standing on the two shoulders they should lean back on the extended rope and the pyramid should be stable. On the water it will help if one of the base carriers uses one hand to hold the arm of the other so that the two skiers do not split apart. The climber should go up like a monkey and grab anything they can to get up there. The water should be reasonable for skiing. It doesn't need to be flat calm, but there should be a straight long enough to get the pyramid built before you start a large radius turn. Use skis as large as possible for the base carriers. You start out all skiing together with the climber in the middle. The climber drops a ski, putting their foot on the thigh of one of the carriers, and then drops the other ski and climbs up. It's very important that if one skier falls, everyone else lets go immediately. That's because flailing ropes can wrap around a skier's legs, and you all want to be together for the next start. Pulling one or two skiers back to one who is in the water is a dangerous manoeuvre. When

19

you want to finish, the climber can either let go and roll back to clear the carriers' skis or climb down and stand on the back of one of the carriers' skis.

It helps if friends in a second boat can follow and pick up the climber's skis before they get run over and then have them ready if you need to start again. Also they will probably want to act as the official camera boat to record your success. If you have a favourite charity you could get your friends to sponsor you if you are successful.

Waterskiing is a family fun sport – enjoy it safely.

20 Recovery and the road

Returning home after a trip out can be confusing because the scene may be different: land that was covered with water earlier is now dry, or vice versa. If it is possible to come alongside a jetty or pontoon, do so and tie up there. This will allow you time to fetch the vehicle and trailer, and assess the situation.

It is not wise to leave a boat on the shore with a falling tide since it could be high and dry by the time you return with the car and trailer from the car park. If there is no jetty, one person must remain with the craft, standing in the water and pushing it gently away from the drying shore.

A boat left on the shore with a rising tide can also create an amusing spectacle for onlookers. As the tide rises the boat will float off – and away – unless one member of the crew stays behind to hold onto it. Alternatively, take the anchor up the beach and make secure.

Whatever the state of the tide, you should always try to avoid beaching the boat, for the hull will swish about with the waves and could be damaged.

Trailer technique

With the boat tied on the jetty, reverse the trailer close to the water and drop the jockey wheel. Attach the towrope to the trailer with a bowline knot and release the trailer from the vehicle.

Push or lower the trailer into the water, until it is deep enough to cover the stern runners or rollers. Experience will dictate how deep it needs to go

Release the strop from the winch and pull it out to nearly the length of the trailer. Take care if the handle is free and spinning. Wait for the handle to lose momentum before you try to stop it spinning.

Take the towrope and connect it to the ball hitch, using a clove hitch. Leave some slack in case the trailer needs to be moved in deeper.

Return to the boat and drive it slowly towards the trailer. Check the wind and tide direction, and aim to arrive slightly to one side of the trailer, so that the boat tends to drift onto the trailer rather than off it. Approach very slowly.

If the engine is on hydraulics, lift the engine just enough for the anti-cavitation plate to be visible, but do not lift it too far or the water-cooling system will fail. Check the water jet for circulation.

When you are getting close, go into neutral, then switch off the engine and lift it fully. Climb over the bow into shallow water and hold the boat. Move the boat into position over the rear of the trailer and connect the strop. Go to the winch handle and swing the trailer to line up with the boat.

20

Trailer deep enough, pull out winch strop   *One crew member stands close to the end of the trailer to guide the hull onto the rollers*

Then winch the boat onto the trailer. A dry member of the crew can then start the vehicle and slowly retrieve the trailer and boat. Once on the flat, the vehicle can be reversed and hitched to the trailer.

Larger craft can sometimes be driven onto the trailer. This requires a very slow approach, and the trailer needs to be deep in the water. It is essential to have two guideposts at the rear of the trailer if you are using this method since the trailer itself is submerged. The posts will also help to line up the approach and will keep the craft central on the trailer. Pipe insulation material wrapped around the posts will help to prevent damage to the boat. A wet crew member can be standing at the back of the trailer deep in the water, ready to receive the bow of the approaching boat. This person guides the boat onto the trailer by hand and connects the winch. Assess the risk and do not stand between the boat and the trailer.

When the craft is on the trailer, go into neutral, switch off and lift up the engine or lower leg. Climb off over the bow, keeping clear of the trailer. Connect the strop and winch up the boat. Signal the driver to slowly tow the boat out. As it starts to leave the water, check the trailer rollers are in position. If one has rolled out of position, return the trailer to deeper water and reposition the roller by hand. But be careful not to trap your hand or fingers between the roller and the hull. Even small waves will lift and drop the hull, with potentially bone-crushing consequences.

If there is a crosswind or cross tide, try to organise a long rope from the stern of the boat to a crew member ashore. This should prevent the stern from swinging away.

With larger, heavier craft, do not rely too heavily on the winch. Try to float the boat as close as possible to the winch itself. Be prepared to get wet and do allow a lot of time for the recovery of a heavy boat.

Note the safety rope holding the bow to the trailer.

20

At some sites there are tractors on standby. On seeing you arrive, a tractor will drive down the slipway with your trailer. This makes life much easier. The tractor driver guides you and does the winching. He then pulls you up the slipway and you do not even get wet feet, although you may prefer to climb out and position the boat on the trailer yourself. At some launching sites they use the hydraulic lift. All you have to do is leave the boat on the jetty and the rest is done for you. Specialised launching could be carried out using a hoist.

Landing in heavy seas

Rescue craft launched from the beach in the surf often have to return to the beach in the same conditions. On lee shores the waves can be very powerful indeed, so the technique is fraught with danger. Understandably, this if often referred to as an emergency beaching. In this example, the boat is a rigid inflatable with a manual-lift outboard engine.

While standing off in the waves, release the lock on the outboard engine and test it to see that the engine will in fact lift (this lock is only needed when going astern). Do not drop the engine back down, since it could relock. Gently position it down.

Depute someone to stay by the engine while you concentrate on steering through the waves and selecting the best moment to turn for the beach. You will need to accelerate to travel as fast as the waves towards the shore. If you travel too slowly, the wave will catch you up and either break over the stern or push the stern off course. Within seconds you will be side on and in imminent danger of being rolled over.

Ignore what is happening behind you and aim for the beach on the plane. As you hit the shallows, cut the engine and shout 'lift' to the crew so they lift the engine as you hit the shore. Then you both jump out, keeping hold of the lifelines, and use the forward momentum to pull the craft forward and up the beach (if you're lucky). Take advantage of the waves to move the boat further ashore. A beach party could have previously placed matting or rollers for your arrival and would also act as a catching party.

From this description it should be obvious that this is no place for the GRP lightweight sportsboat. Lee-shore beaching is serious stuff, and should only be attempted by an experienced crew in a powerful, sturdy boat.

20

Taking to the road

Trailing the boat can be a worrying business as you wonder whether the straps will hold and whether something will come adrift or even fall off half way home. It's worth taking the time to make everything secure.

1   Check that all the rollers and supports are correctly placed and that all the nuts are tight.

2   Grease the wheel hub bearings and try them for side movement. If they are loose, readjust or replace them.

3   Tie down the bow from the D-ring to the trailer. Use adjustable ties or strops for securing the boat to the trailer. Make them tight. Pad them out with pieces of carpet where they make contact with the GRP hull and tension them well.

4   If the boat has an outboard, lock it up on the locking lever and place the propeller bag over the lower leg of the engine. This is a legal requirement. Often the locking lever is not strong enough, so insert a block of wood and lower the engine hydraulically back down onto the wood – attach the rope strop to the wood.

5   Attach the trailer lighting board, connect the plugs and check the lighting. Secure the lighting wire to keep it clear of the road.

6   Lift the jockey wheel and make it secure, well clear of the road. Clamp it hand-tight only; if you use your foot you may strip the thread.

7   Lock the trailer to the ball hitch on the vehicle if possible. Connect the automatic brake wire if fitted. If the trailer should break loose, this will automatically apply the brakes on the trailer. Check the tyre treads and pressures, visually at least.

8   Check and secure anything that is loose in the boat, as this could cause damage in transit. Be sure to secure the fuel tank and batteries.

9   Think twice about putting on the boat cover if you are going to be travelling at speed. The wind could tear it to pieces.

10 Walk around the whole rig and check it over from a distance, asking yourself whether you have missed anything.

Essential check

Move out onto the open road and, after a few miles, find a place to stop. Recheck all the ties and the position of all rollers and supports. Recheck tyres and suspension.

Acknowledgements

I have been assisted in my research by Mr John Kilhams, MSMI. John has worked in the boat business for many years and is a qualified marine surveyor. Also, Robert Owen, marine engineer.

David Edmund Jones took the photographs for this new edition in Chichester Harbour and I am grateful to the Chichester Harbour Master and his staff, the Chichester Harbour Conservancy, Lansdale Marine and Honda for all their assistance and generosity.

Nick and Caroline Tomkins generously loaned their boat, time and expertise to be photographed aboard their Monterey, *Avispa*.

Other photographs and original sketch ideas by Peter White

With thanks to Davis Sale of the South Western Ambulance Service NHS Trust for his assistance in the rewriting the first aid chapter.

Many thanks to Robin Nichols for providing the waterskiing section.

Peter White was the founder of the Seafever Powerboat Club, now named "Pathfinder". It remains a very successful cruising club for small sportsboats and RIBs in the UK.

http://www.pathefinderpowerboatclub.org.uk/

With grateful thanks to Wajahat Latif for his wise counsel.

This book is a tribute to my many former students, whose constant questioning and bemused expressions inspired me to put pen to paper.

This book is dedicated to my wife, Hilary Claire, for her total support and unending drive and enthusiasm, which spurred me on during many late nights.

20